THANKS FOR THE DOWNLOAD

LET ME KNOW YOUR THOUGHTS WITH A
REVIEW ON THE WEBSITE.

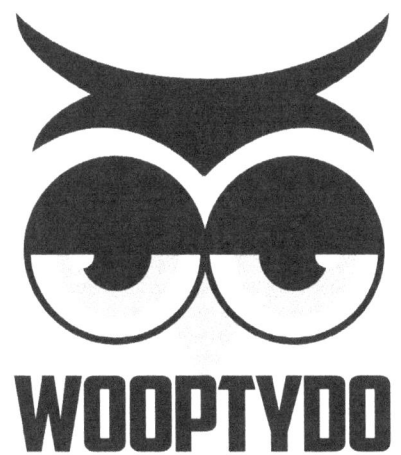

WOOPTYDO

1

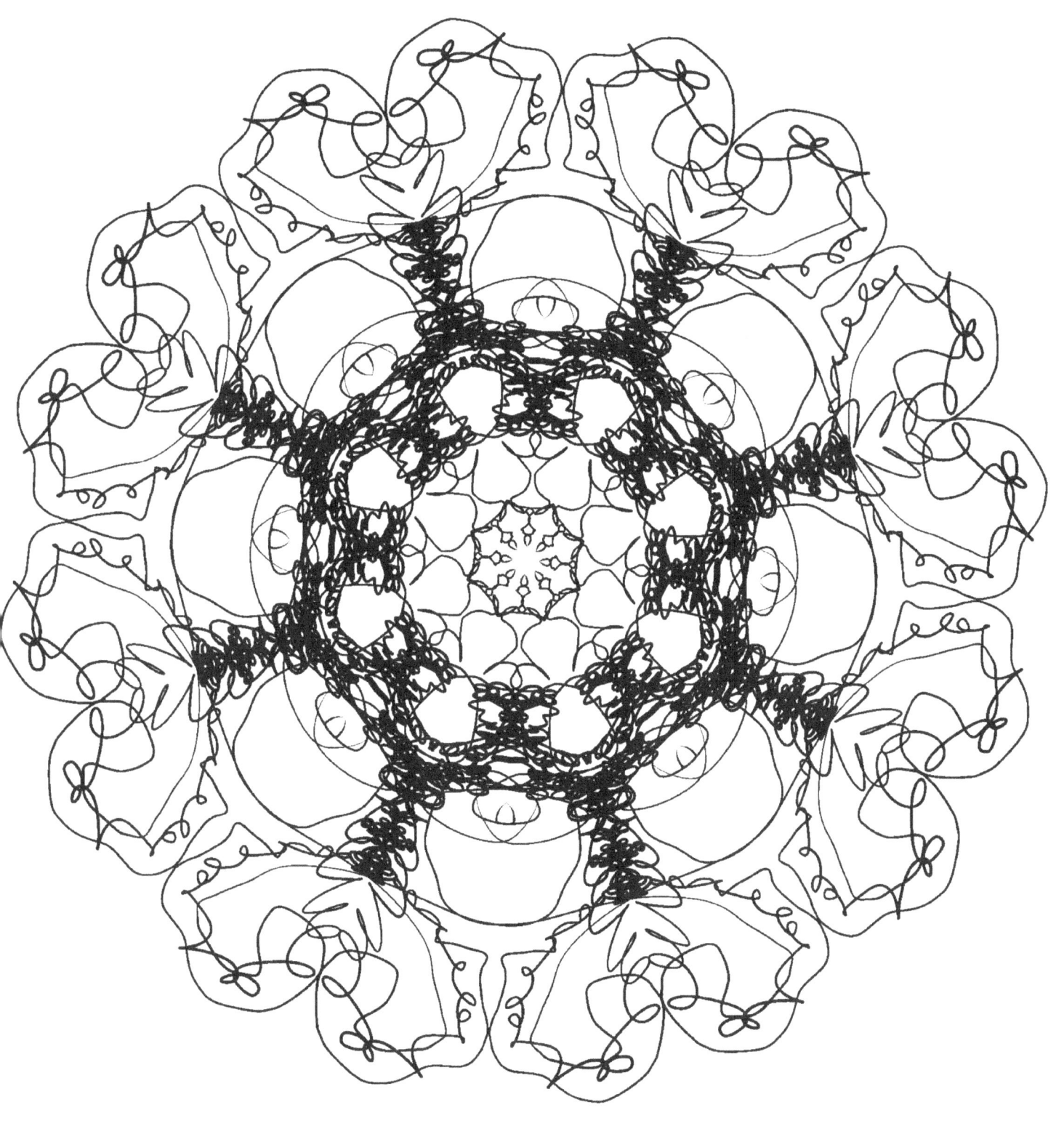

3

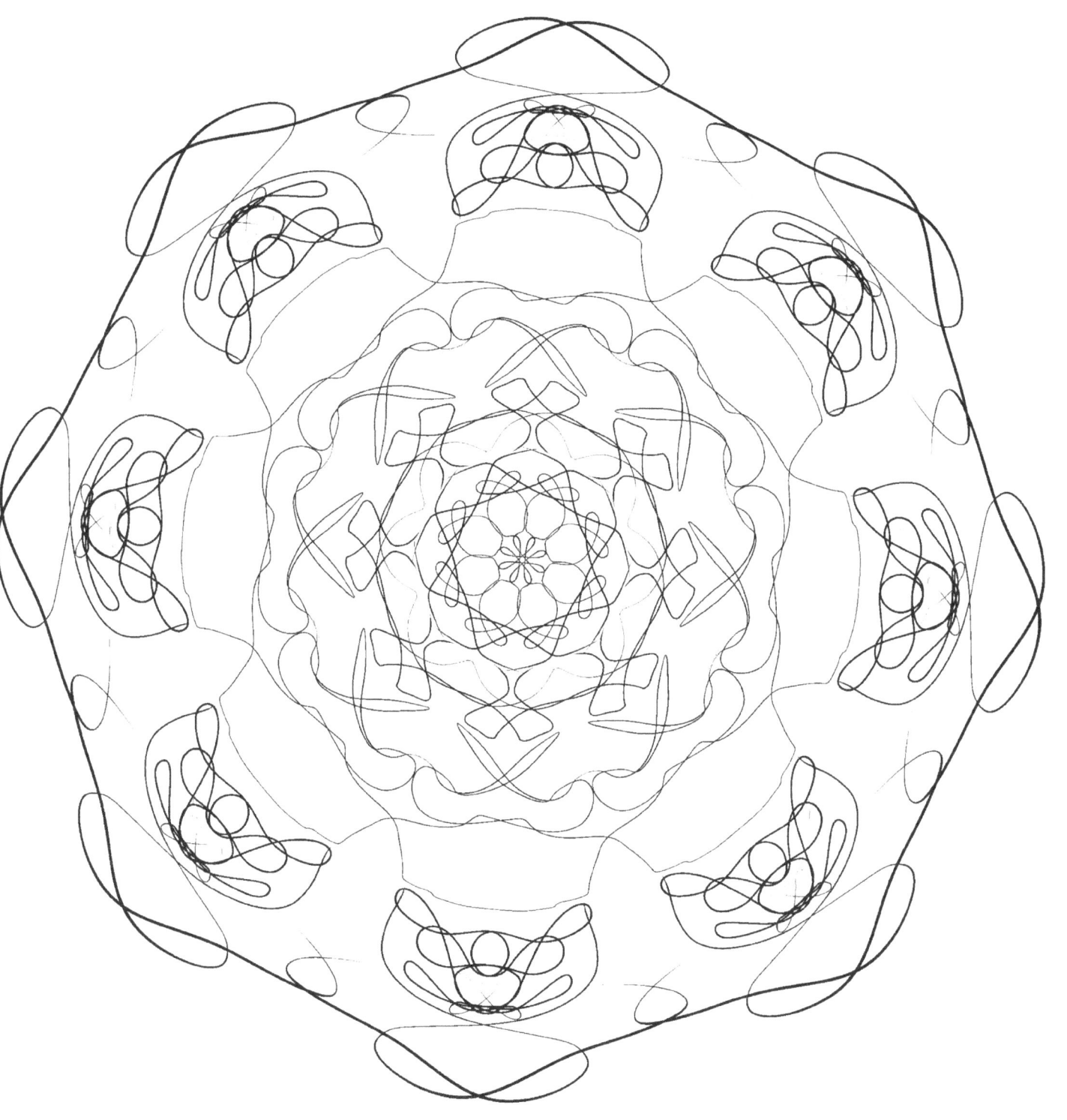

5

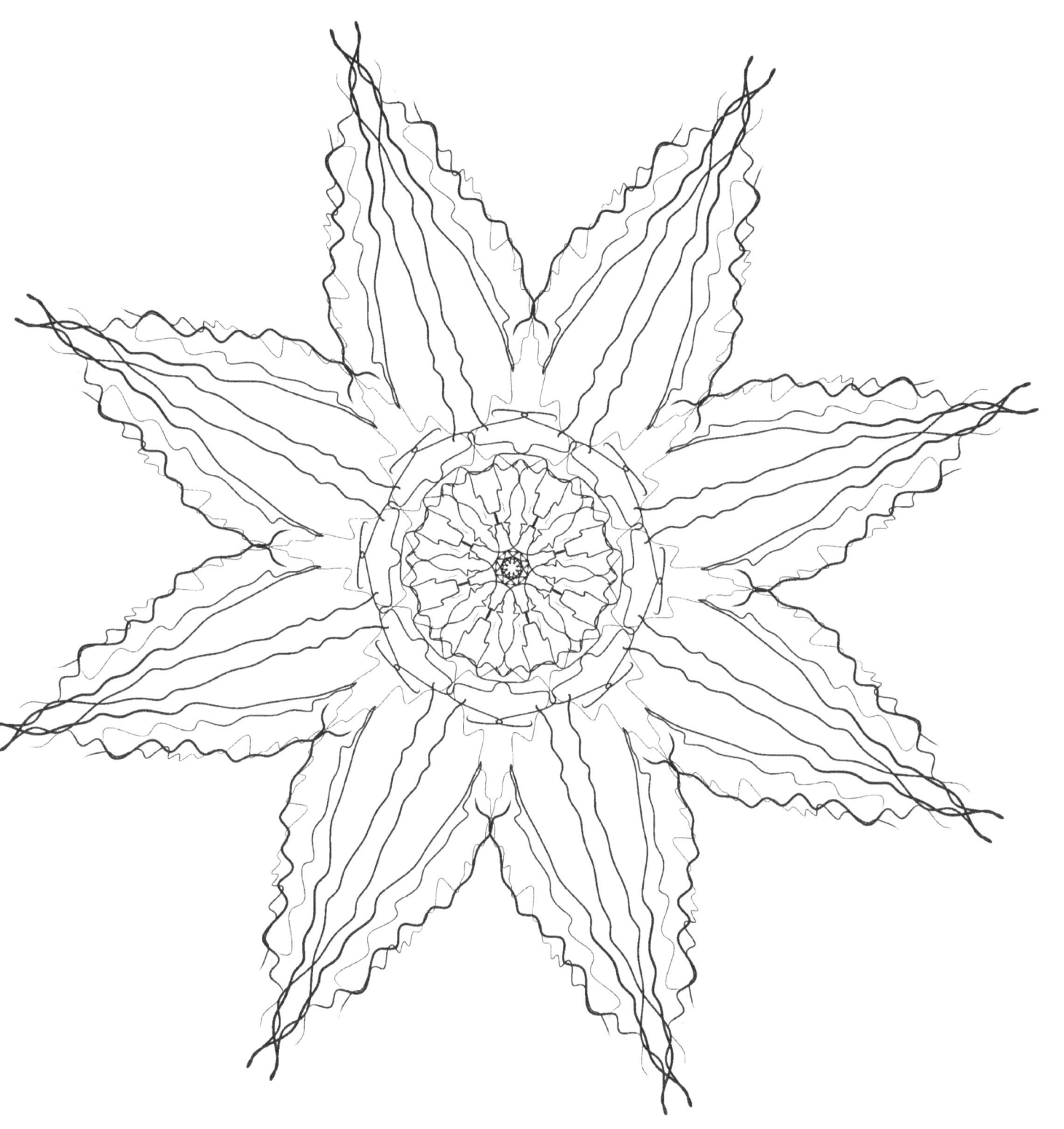

7

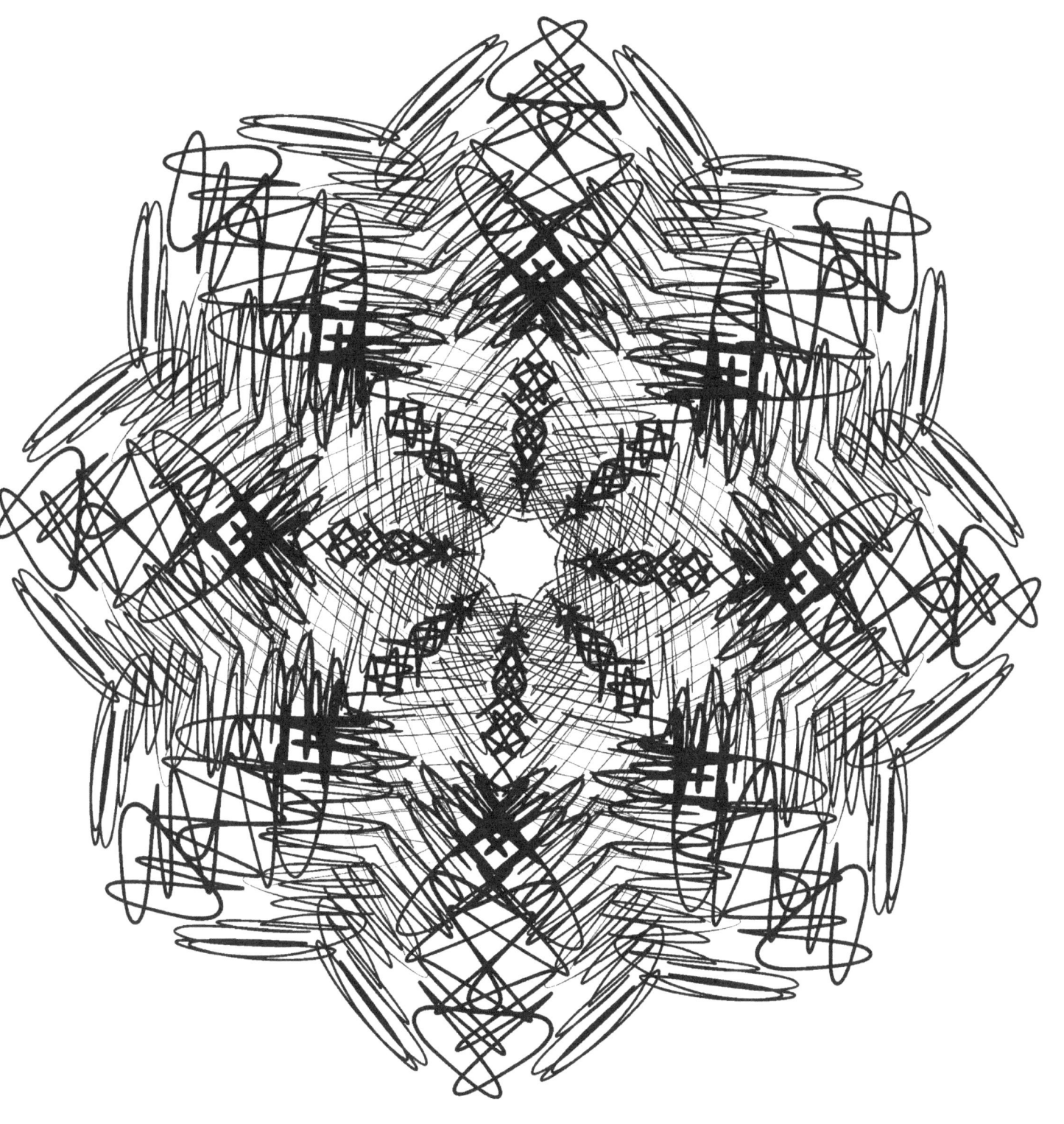

9

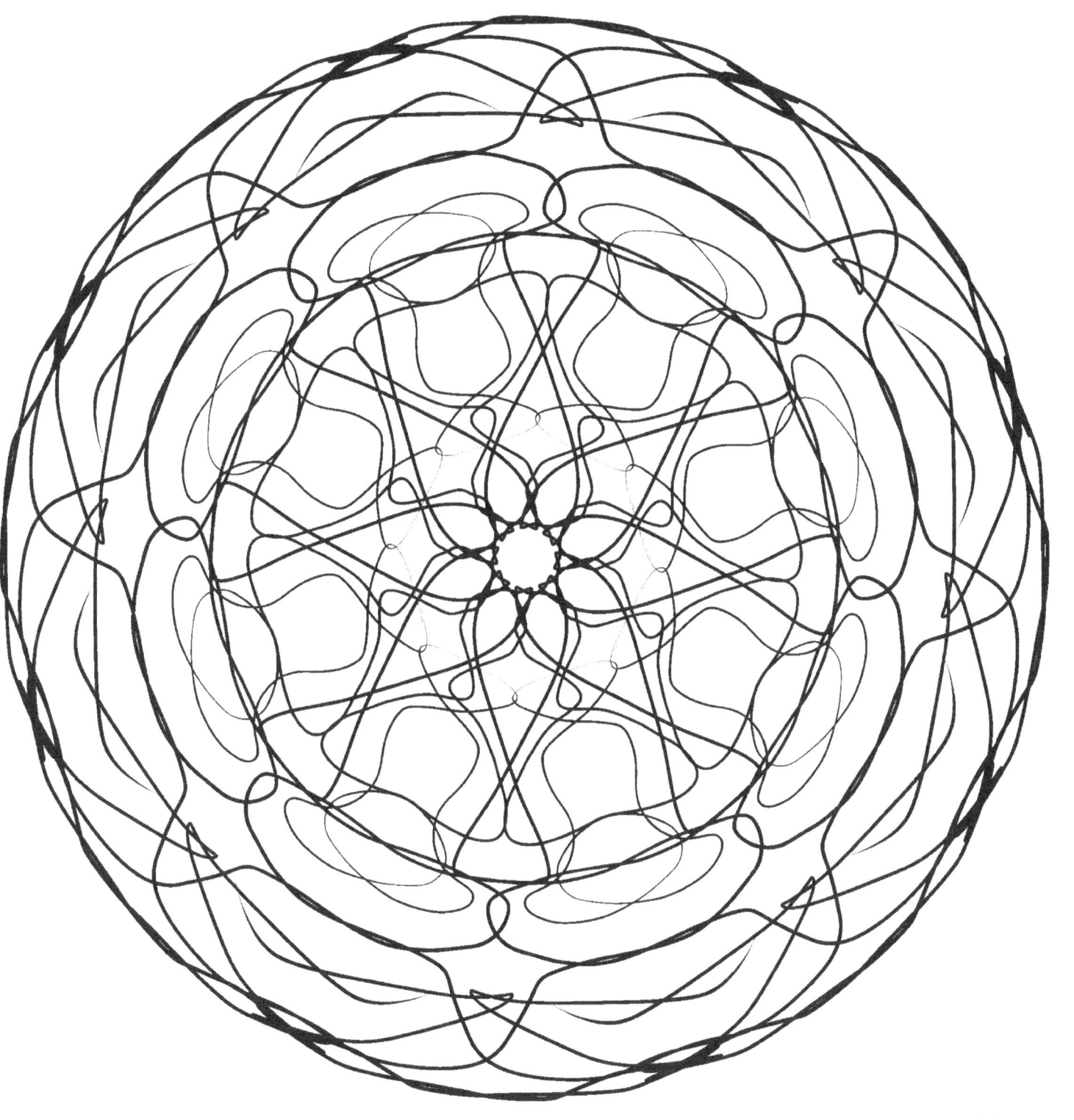

11

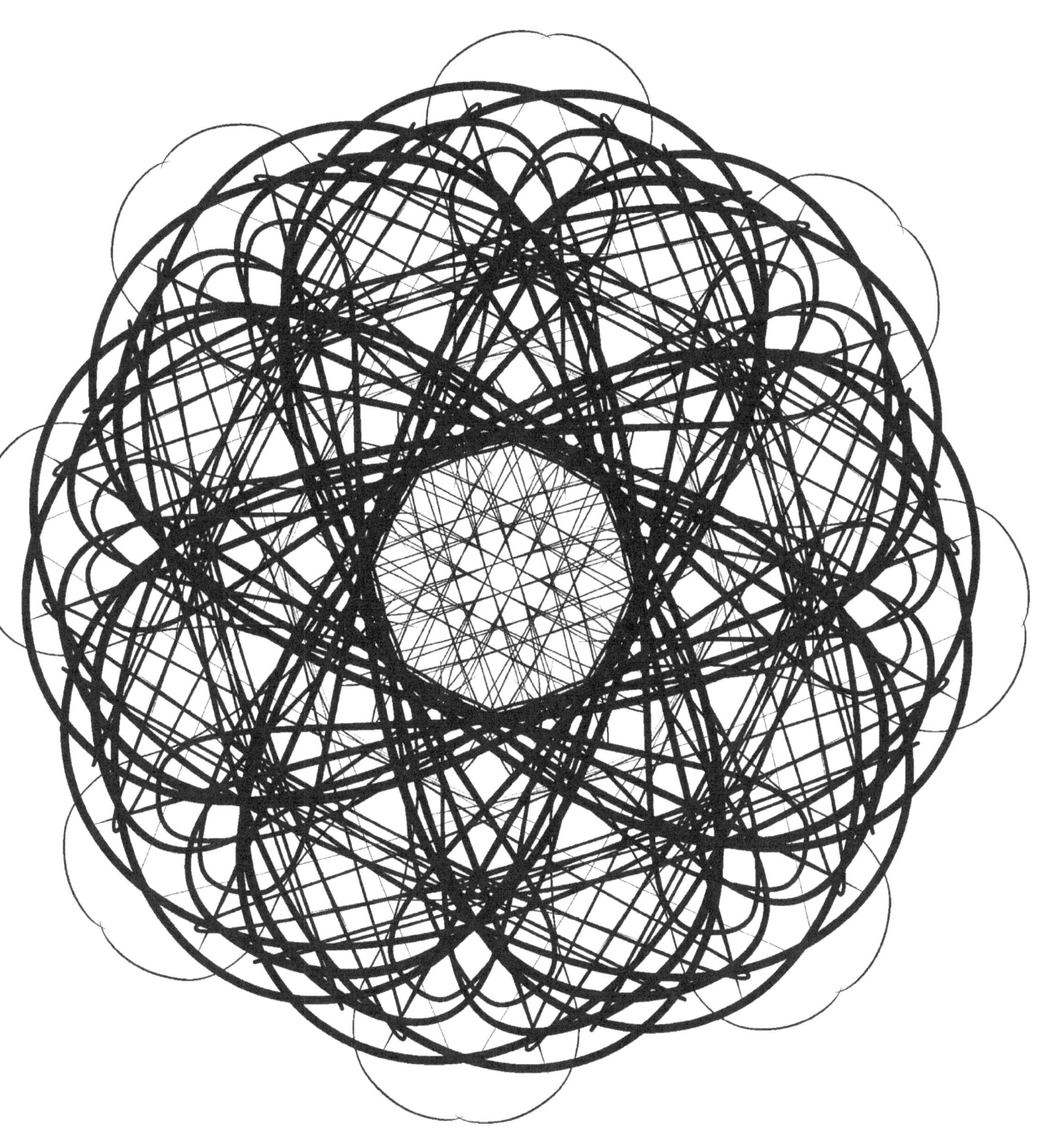

13

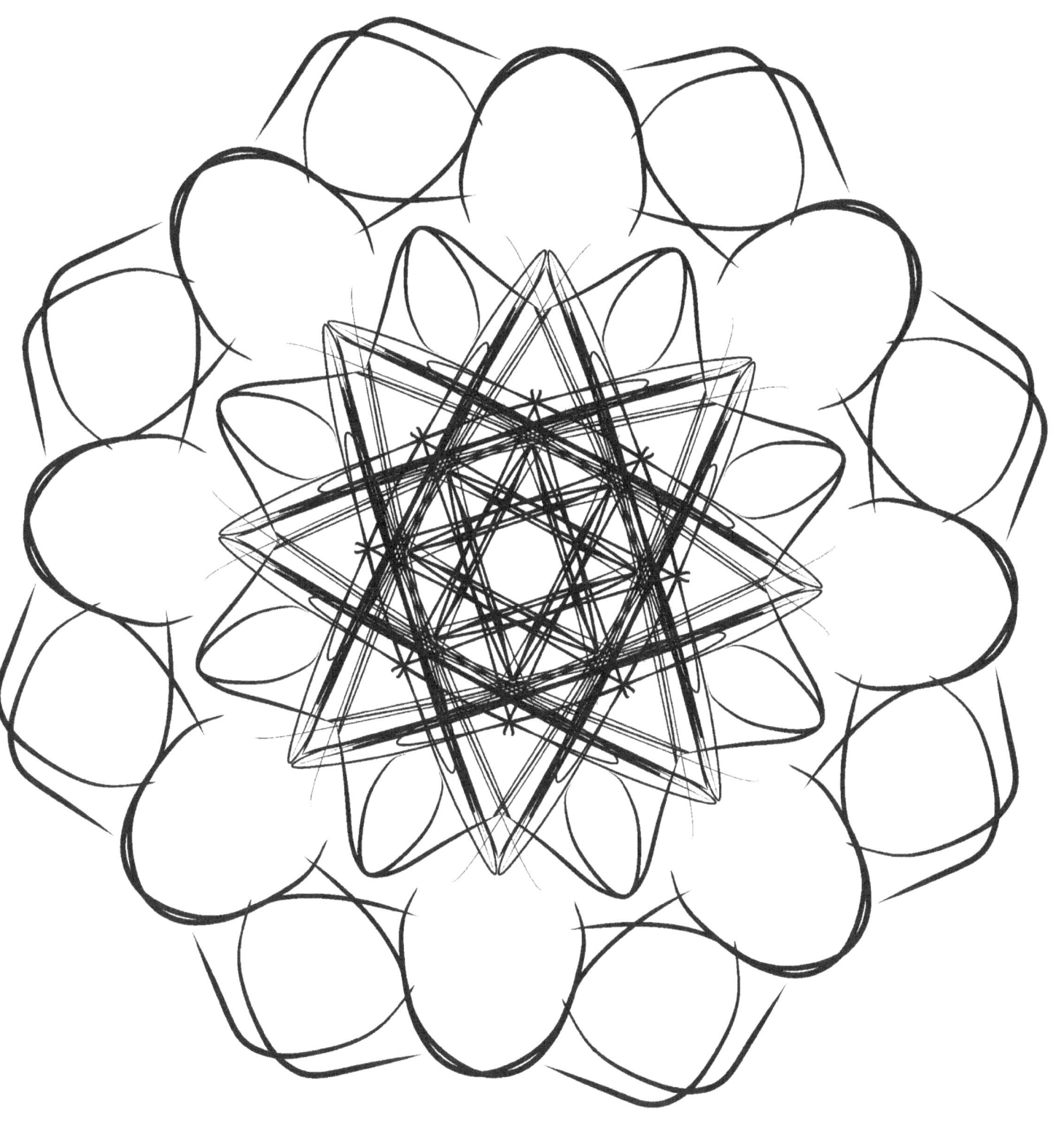

15

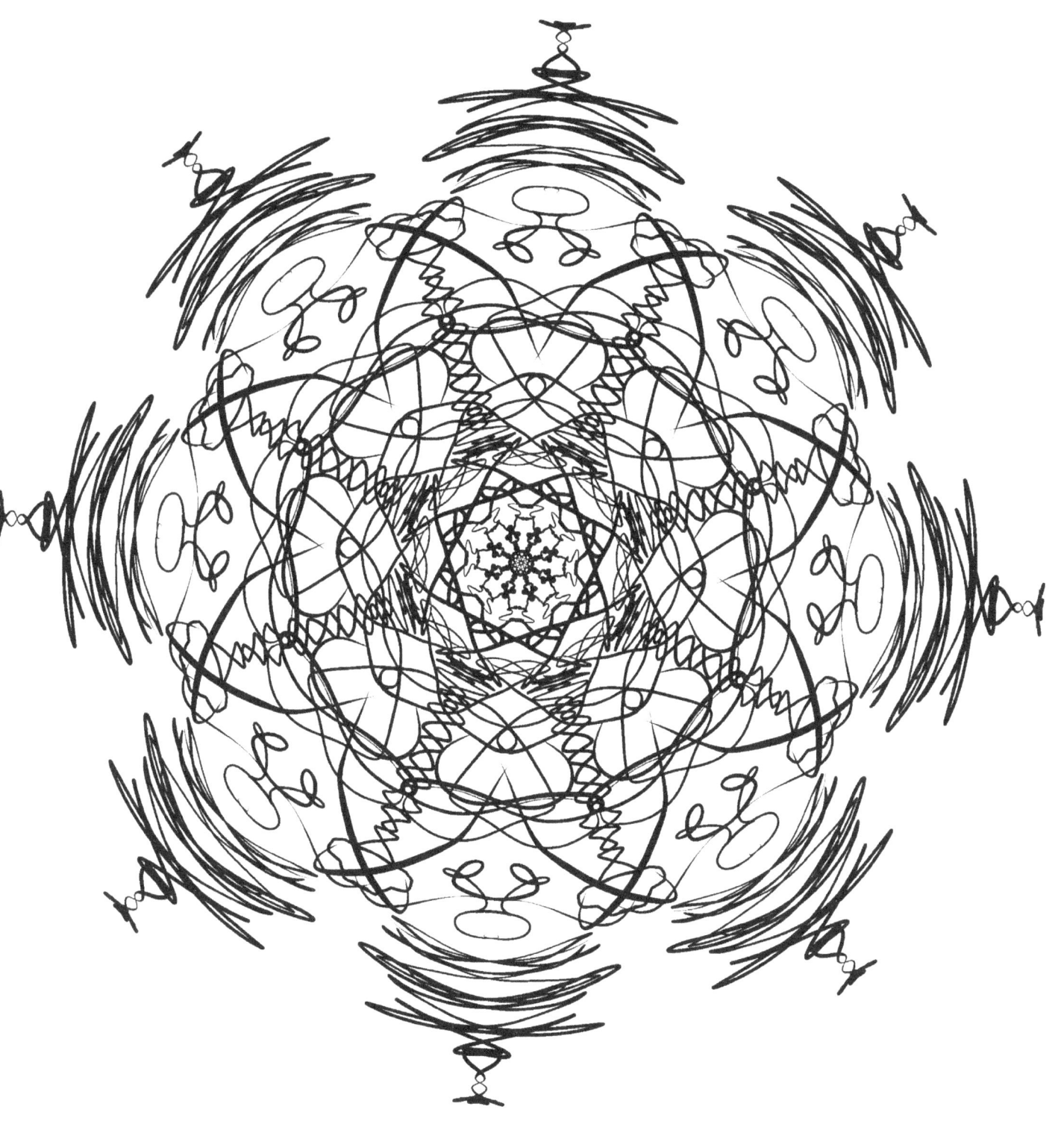

17

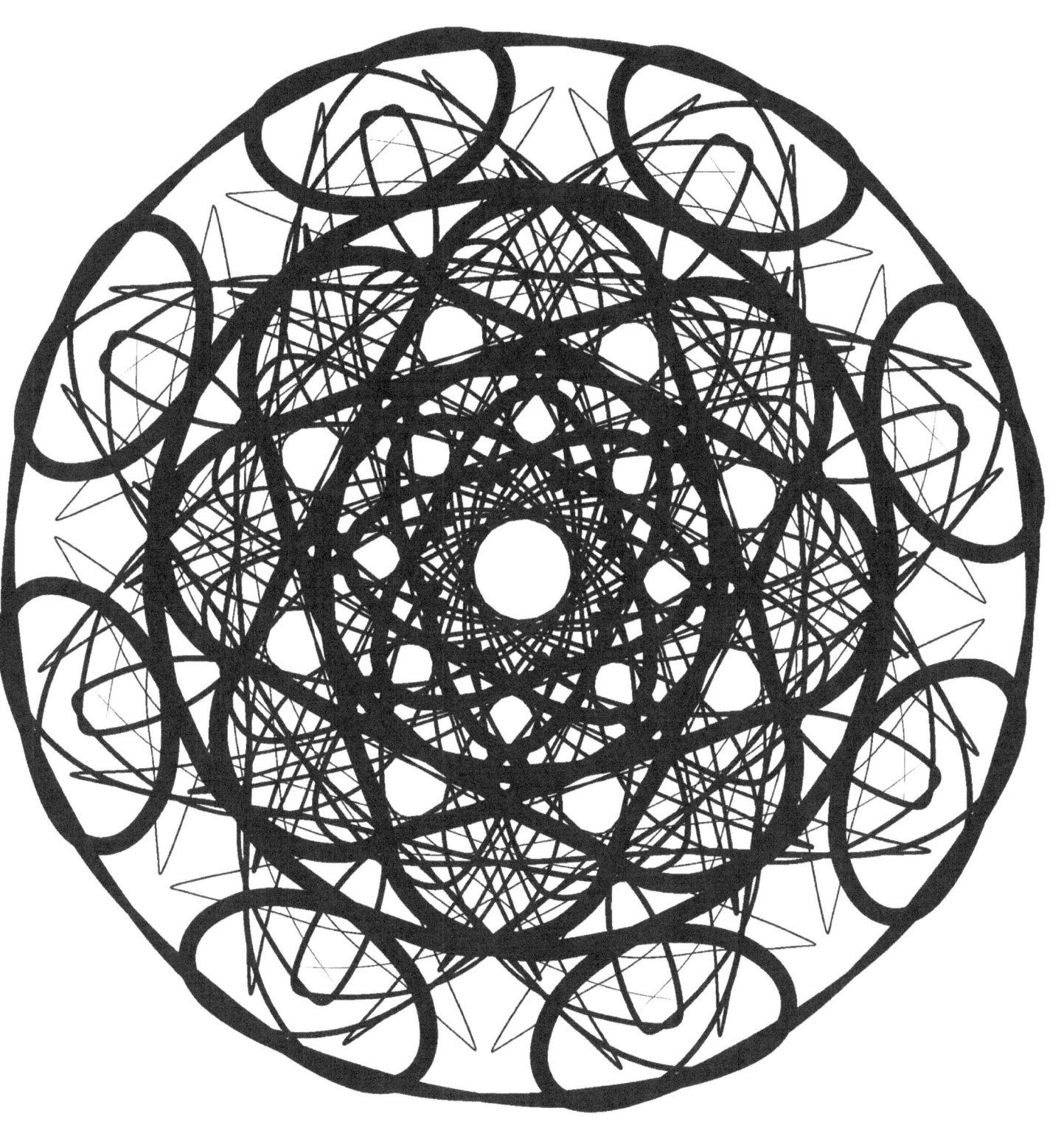

19

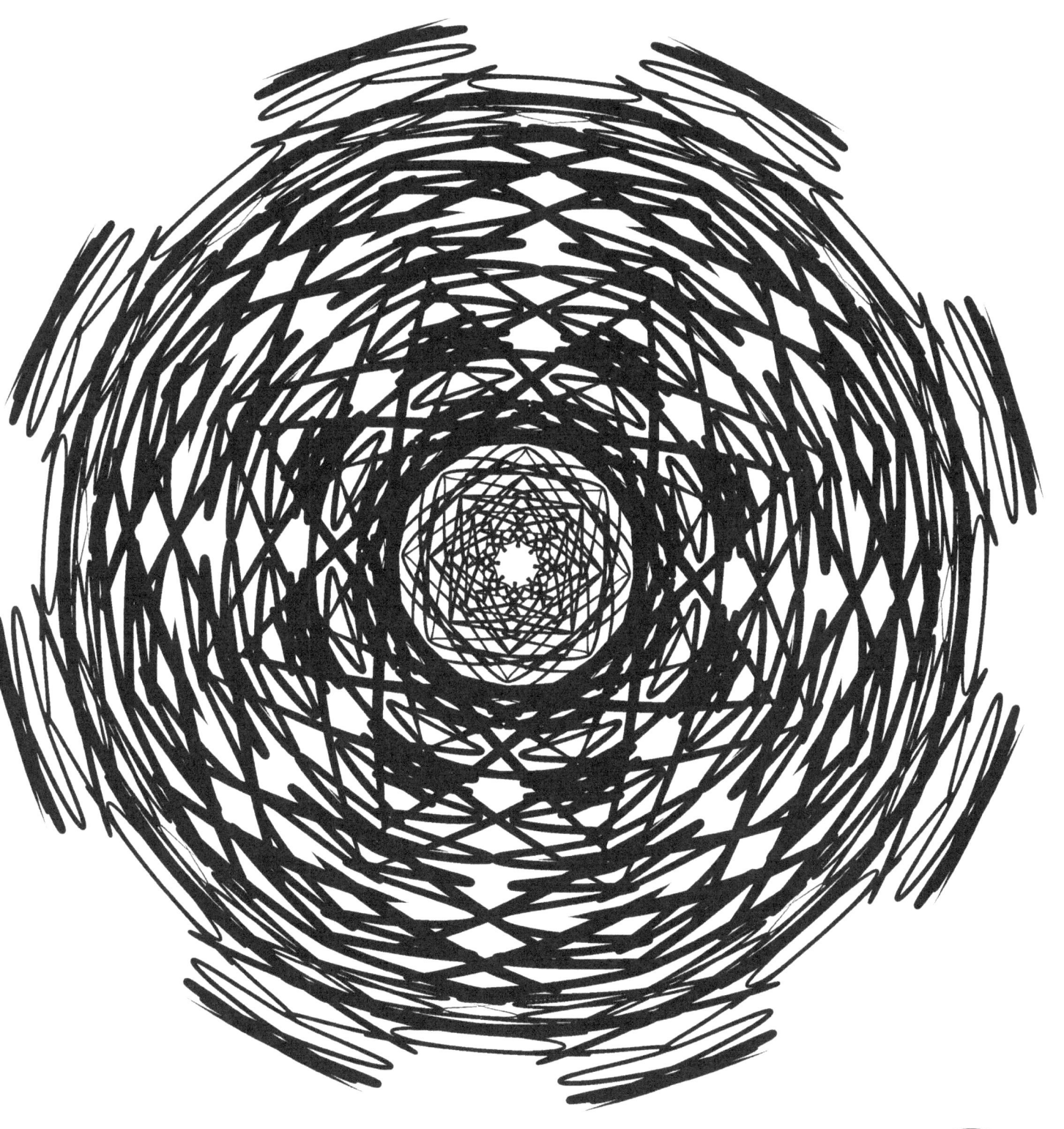

21

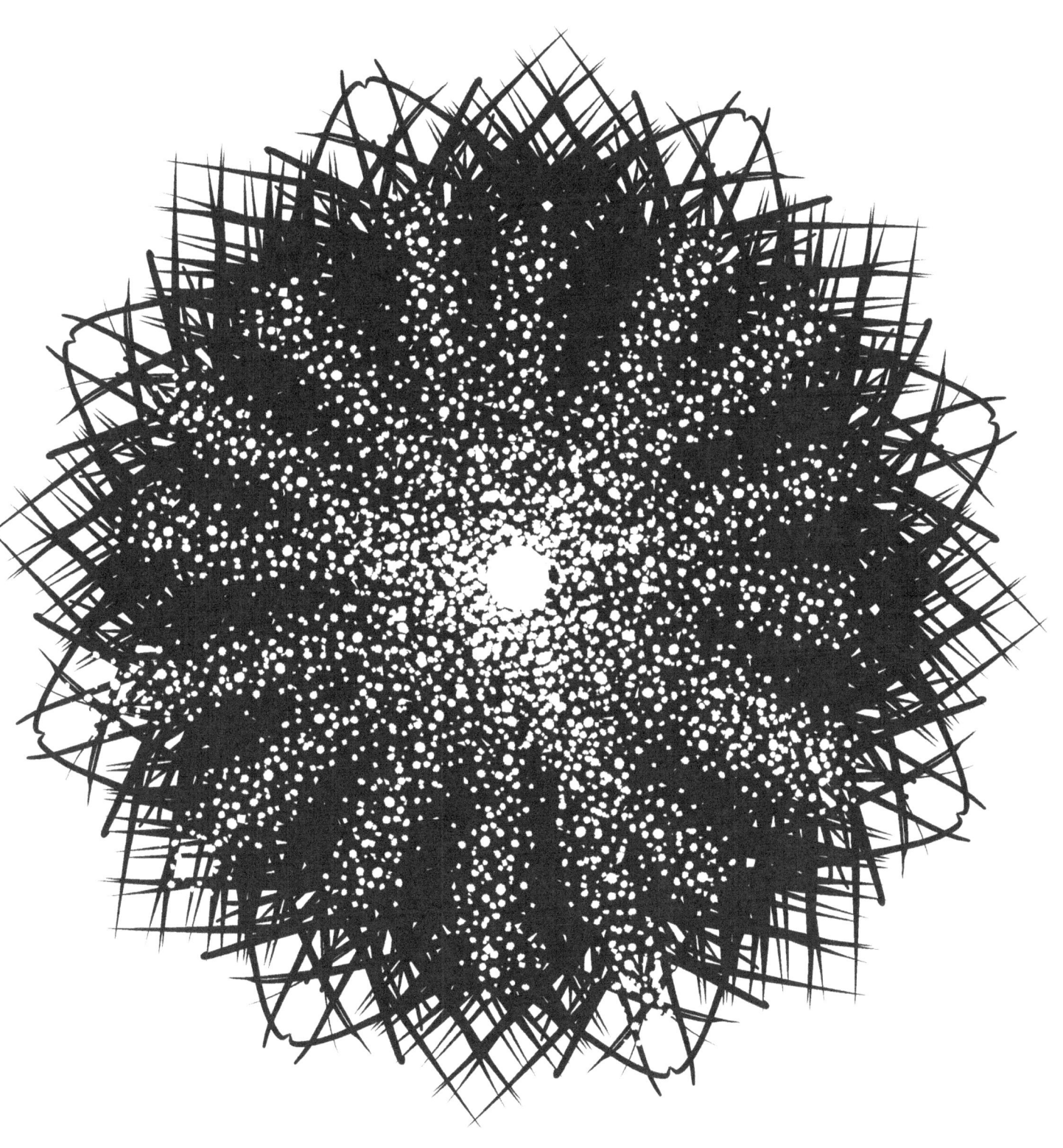

23

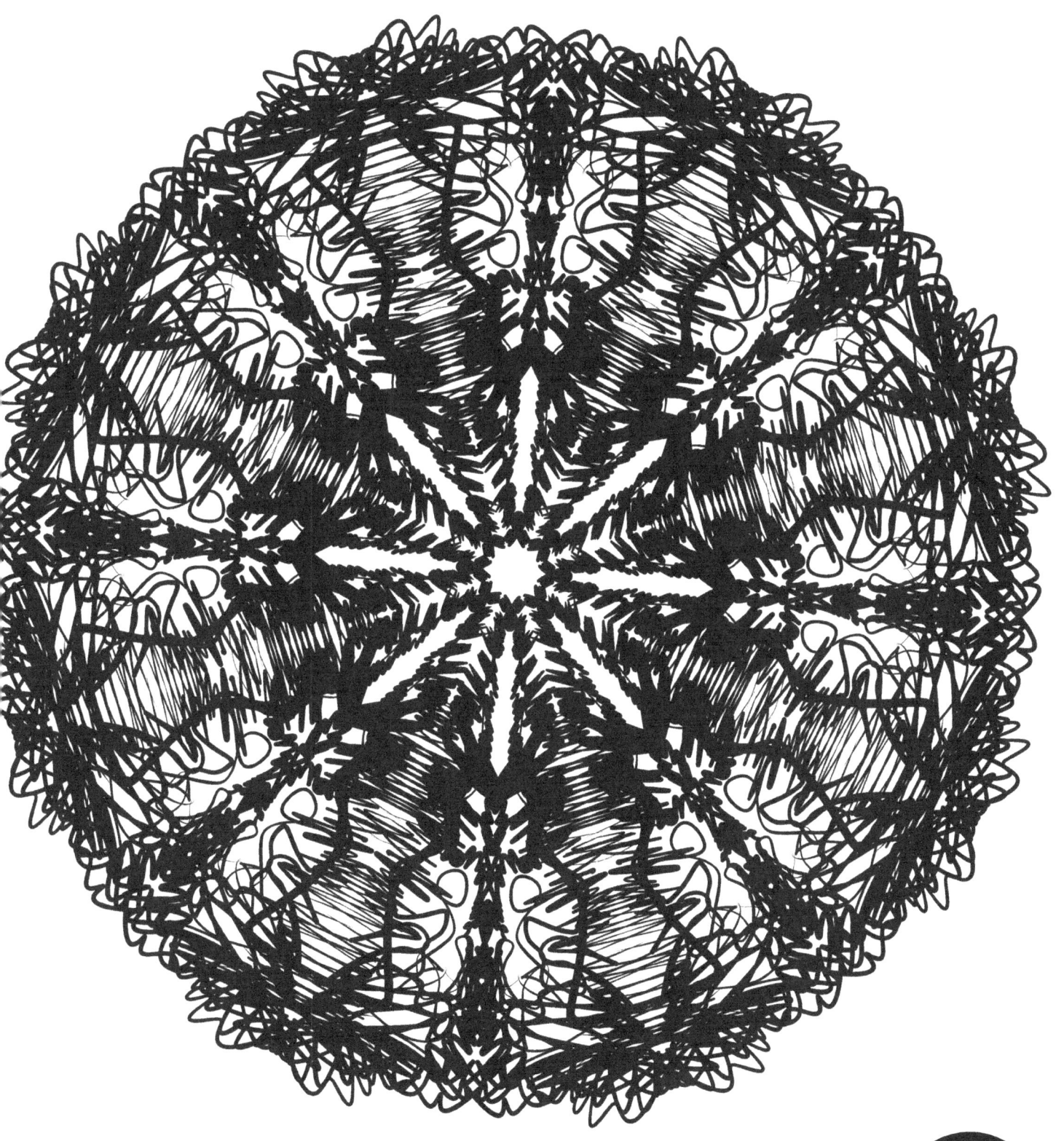

25

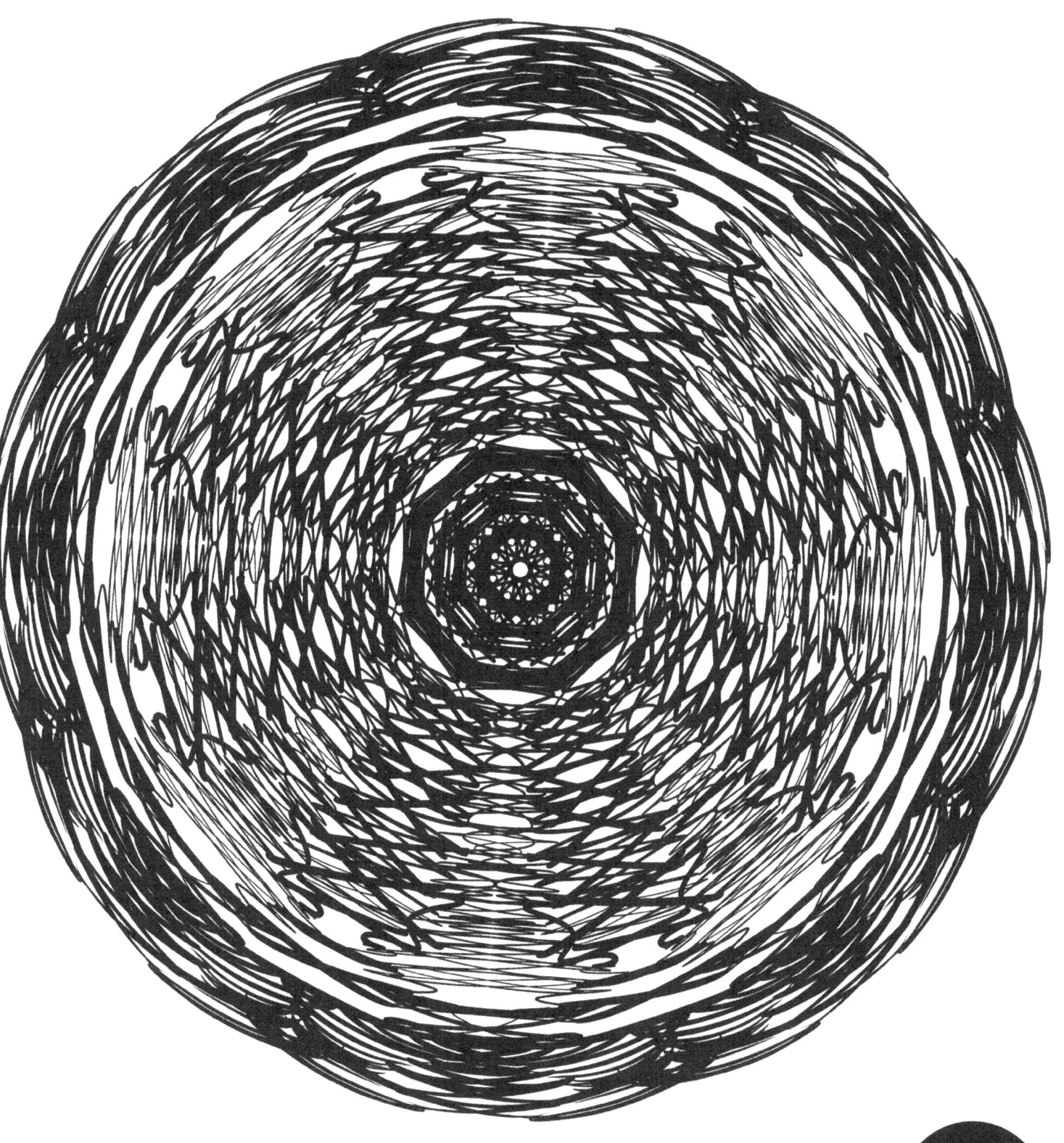

27

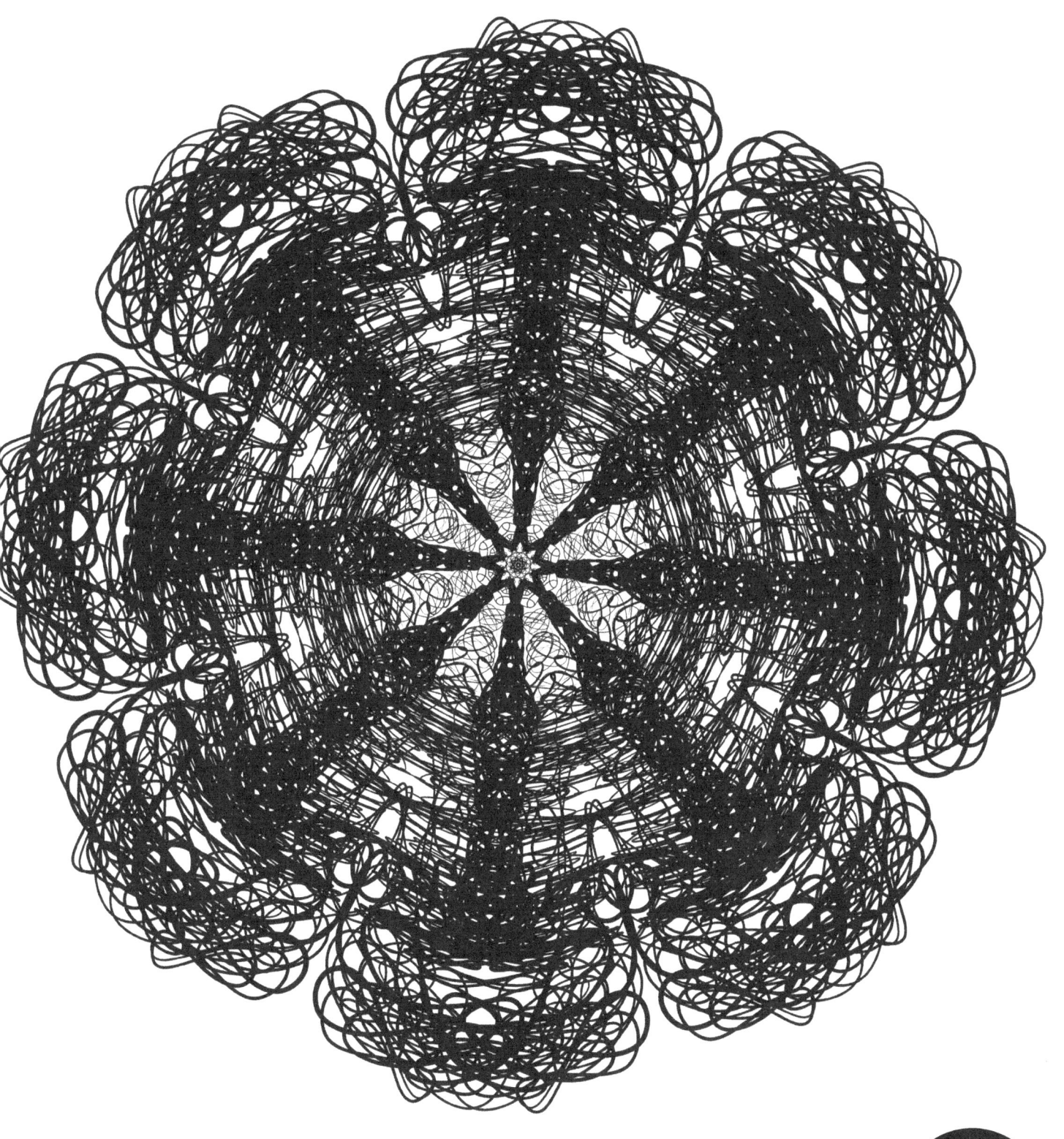

29

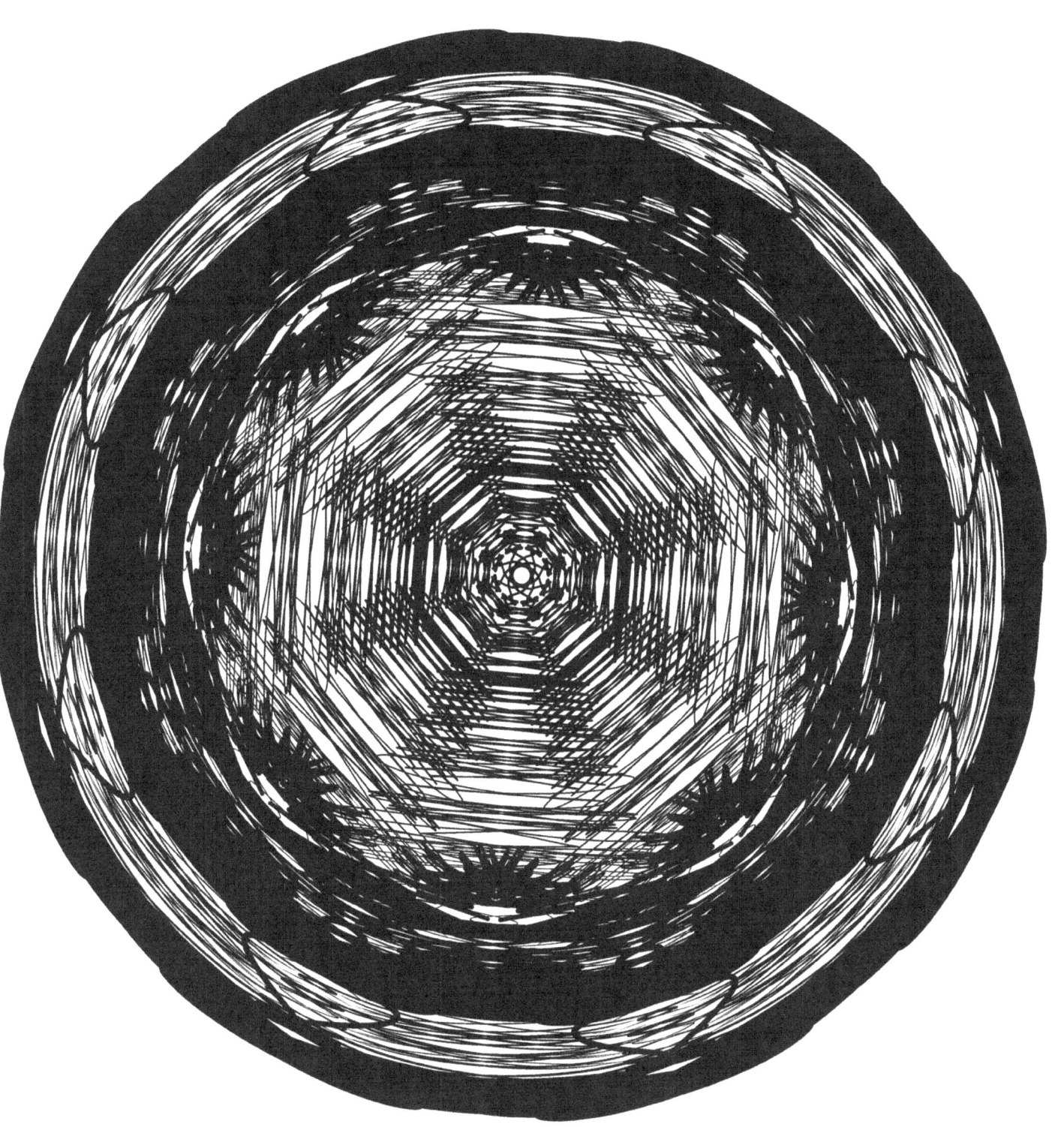

31

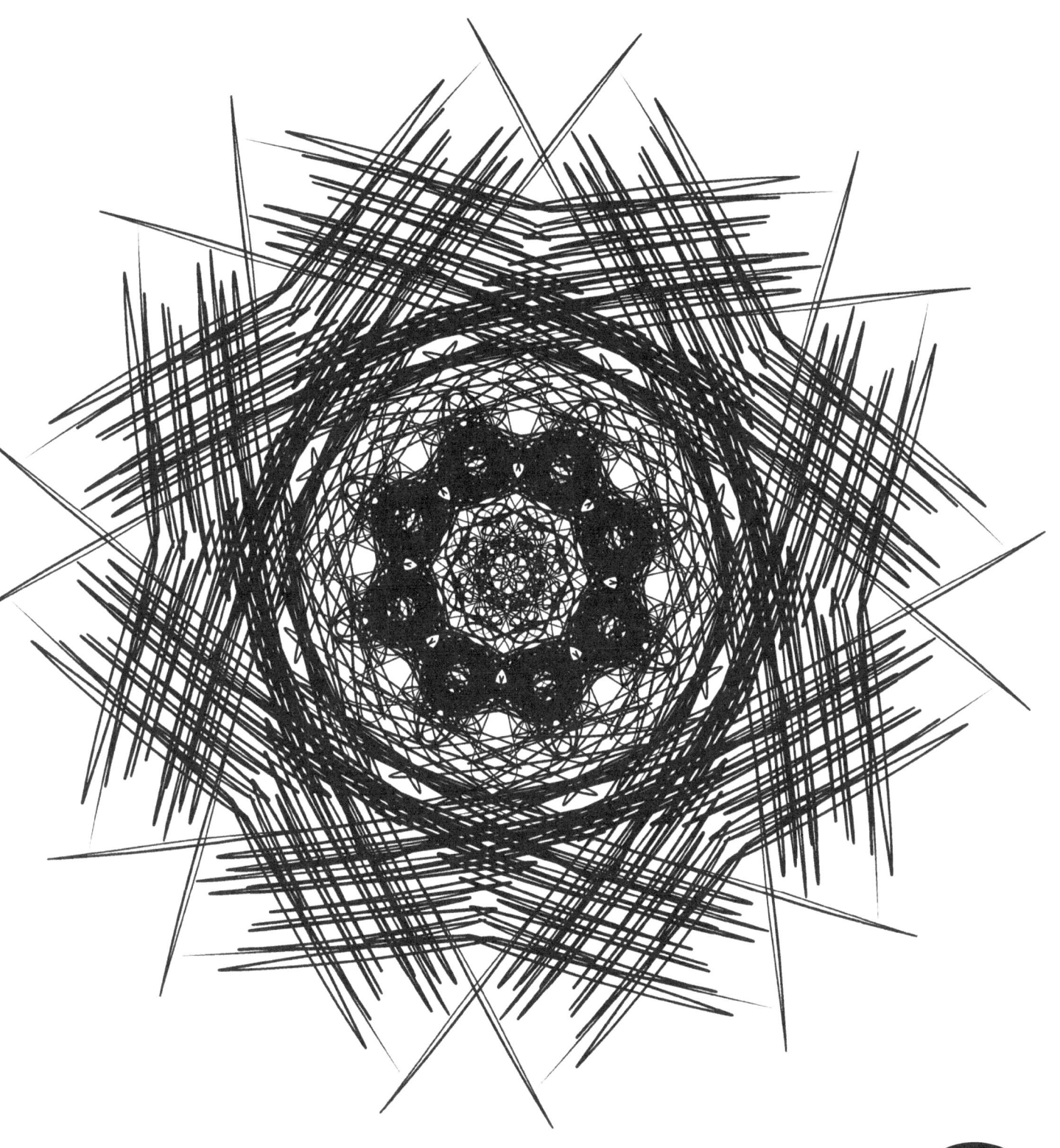

33

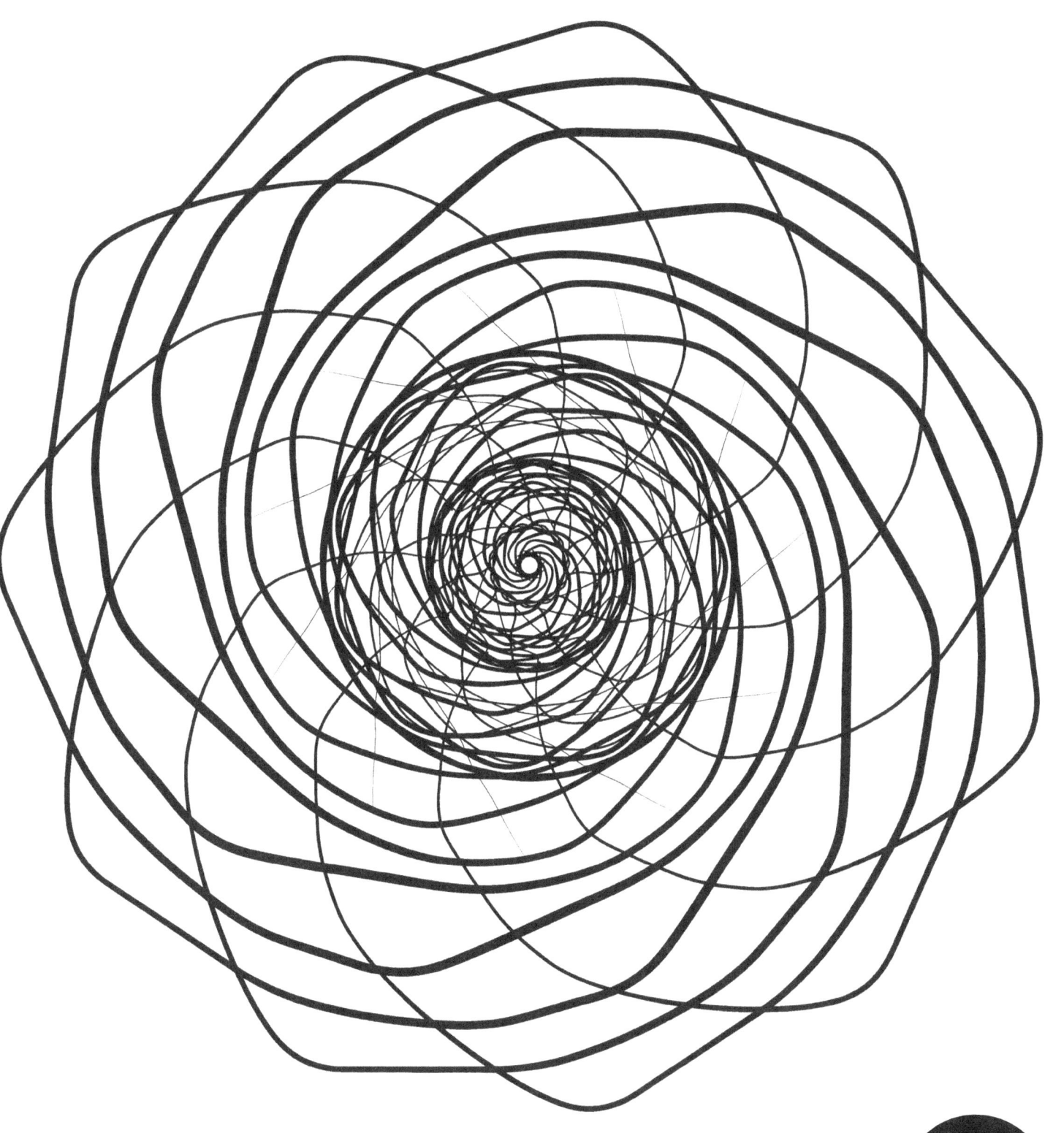

35

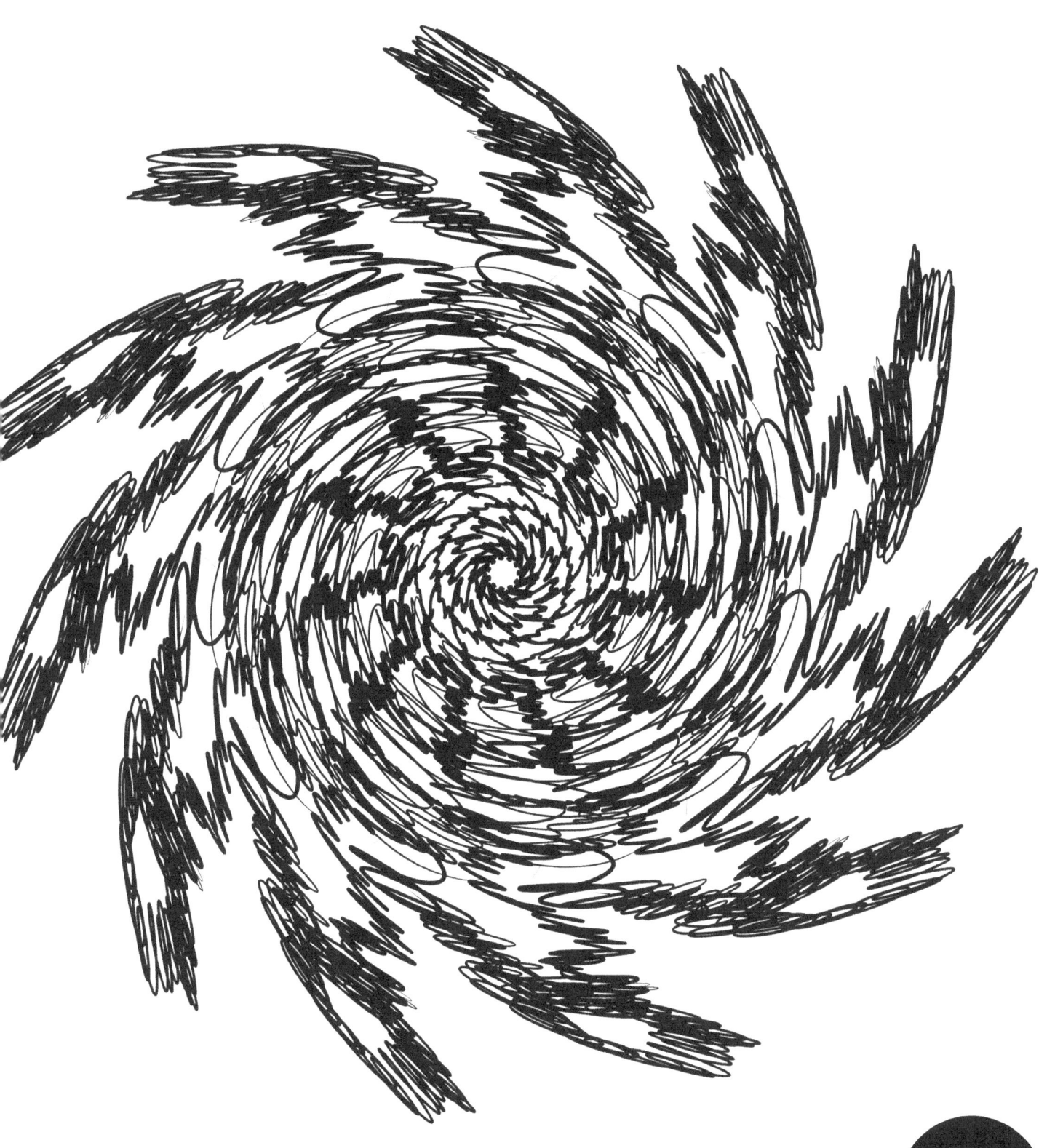

37

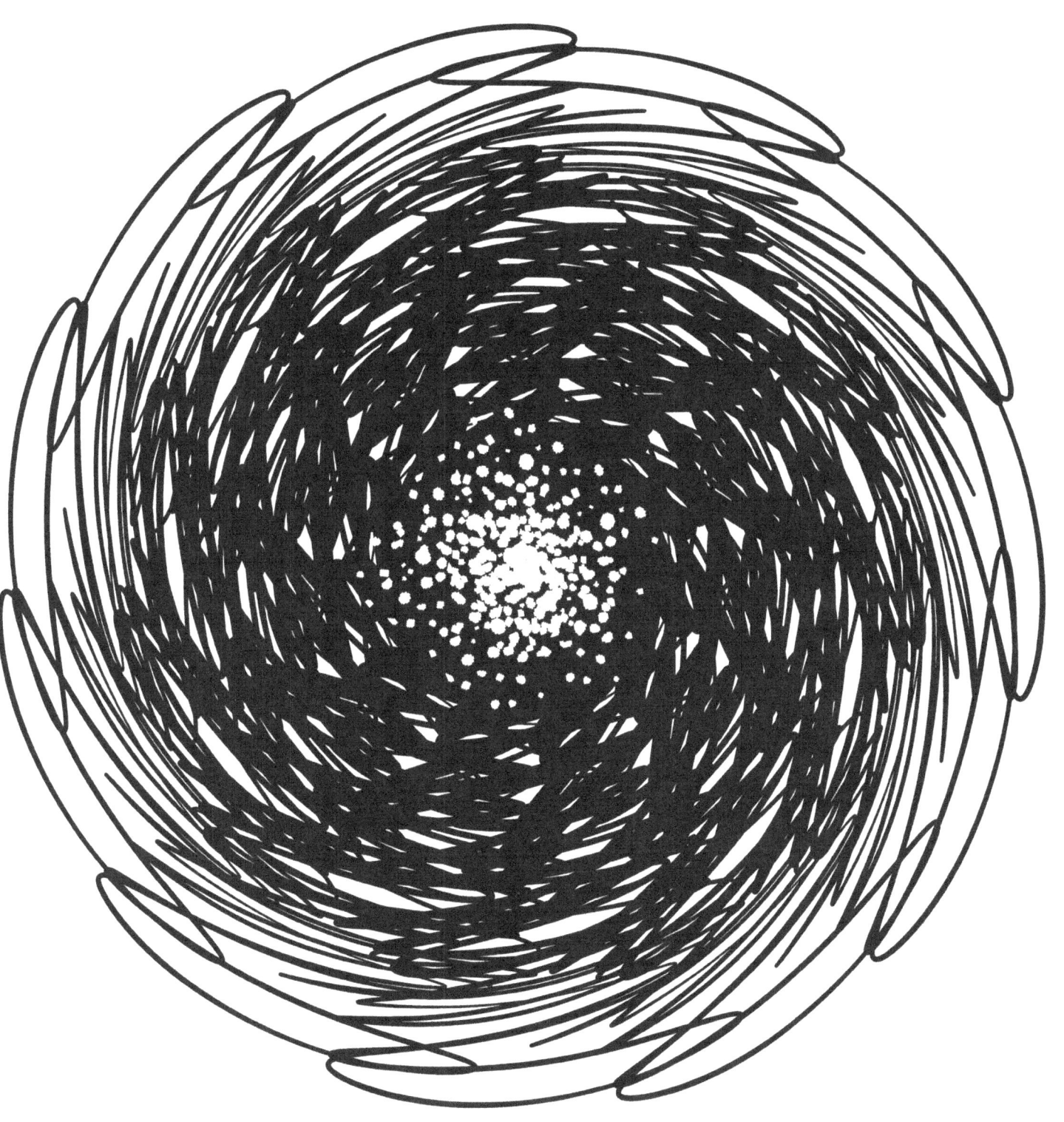

39

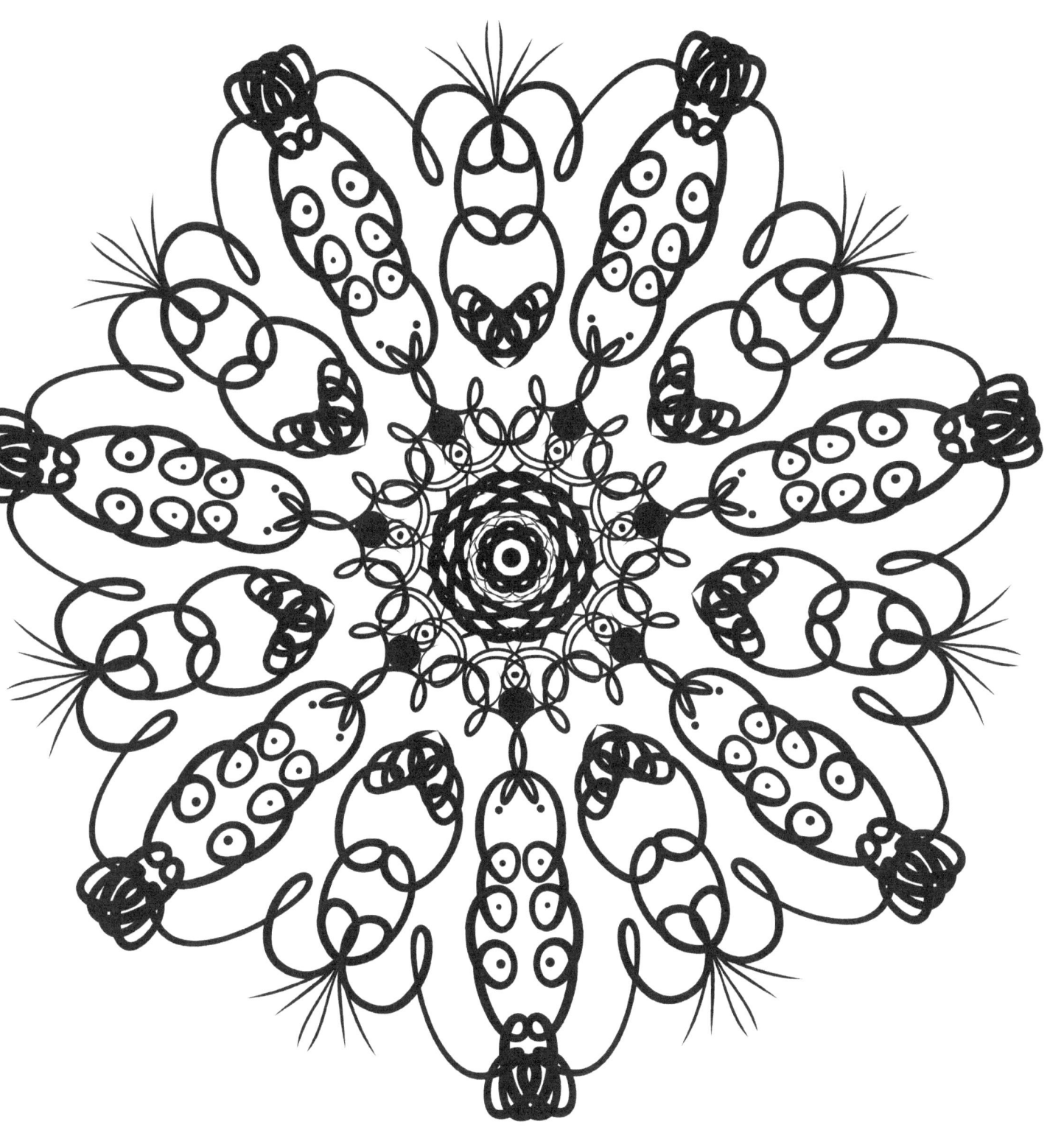

41

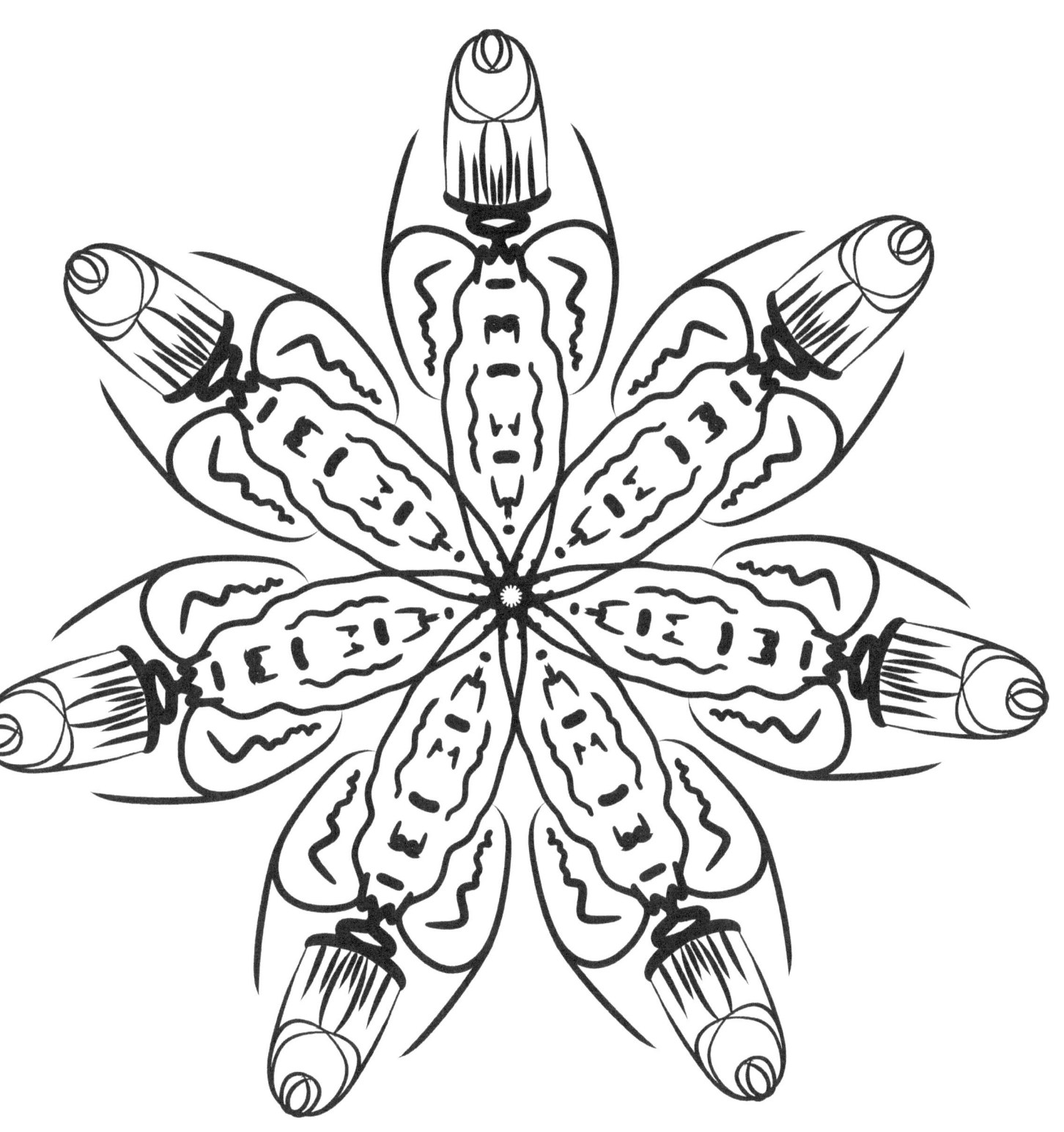

43

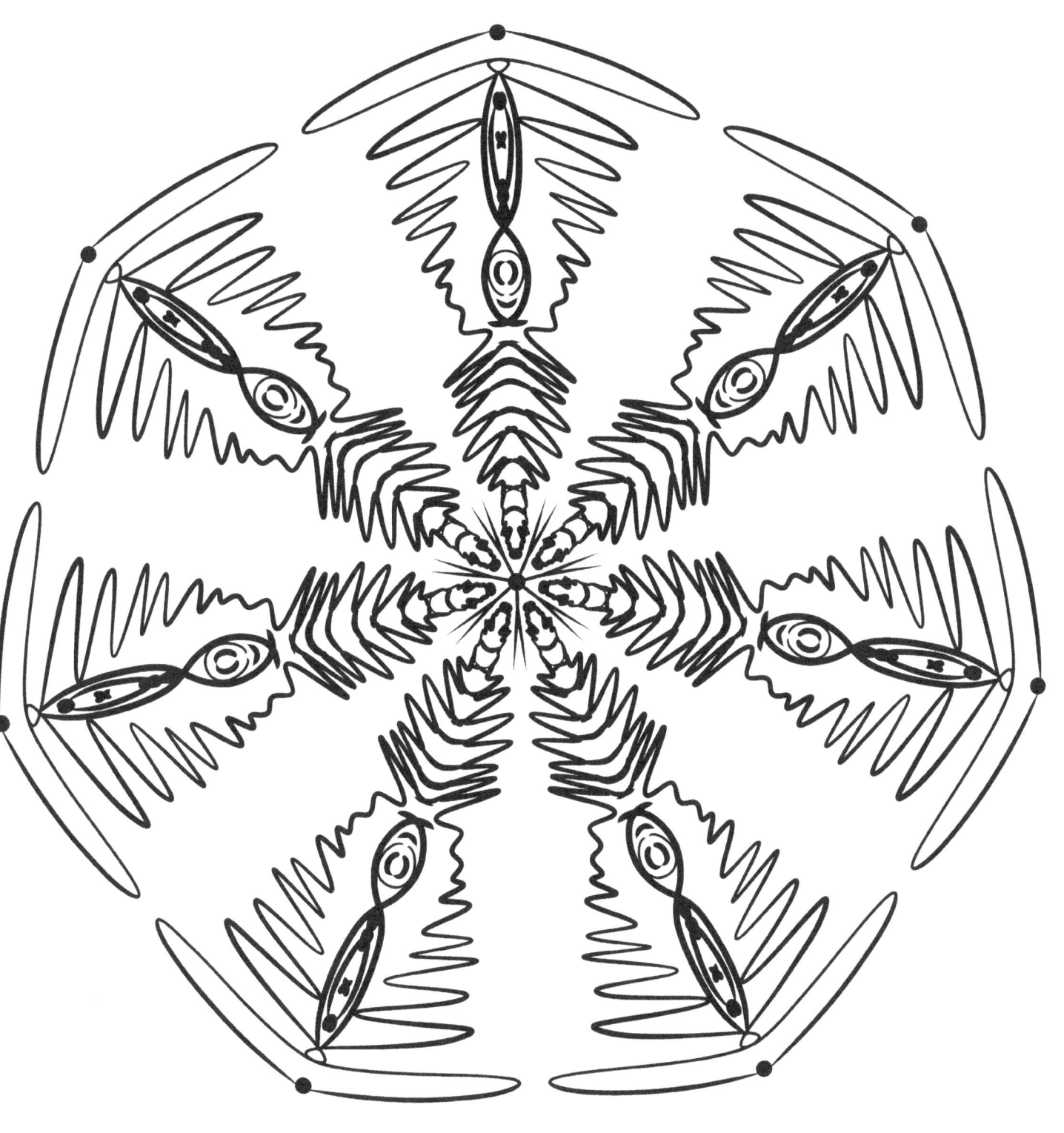

45

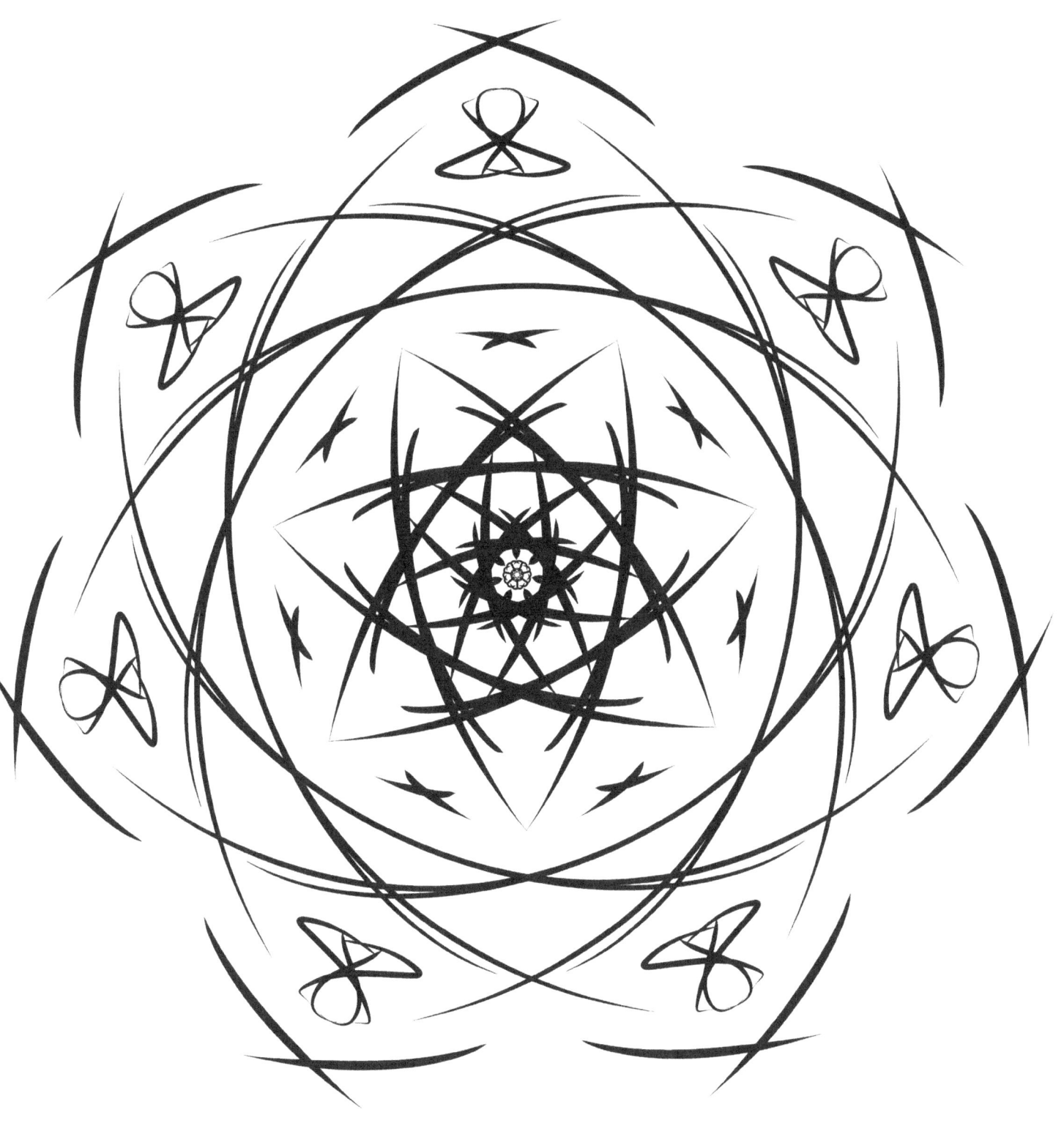

47

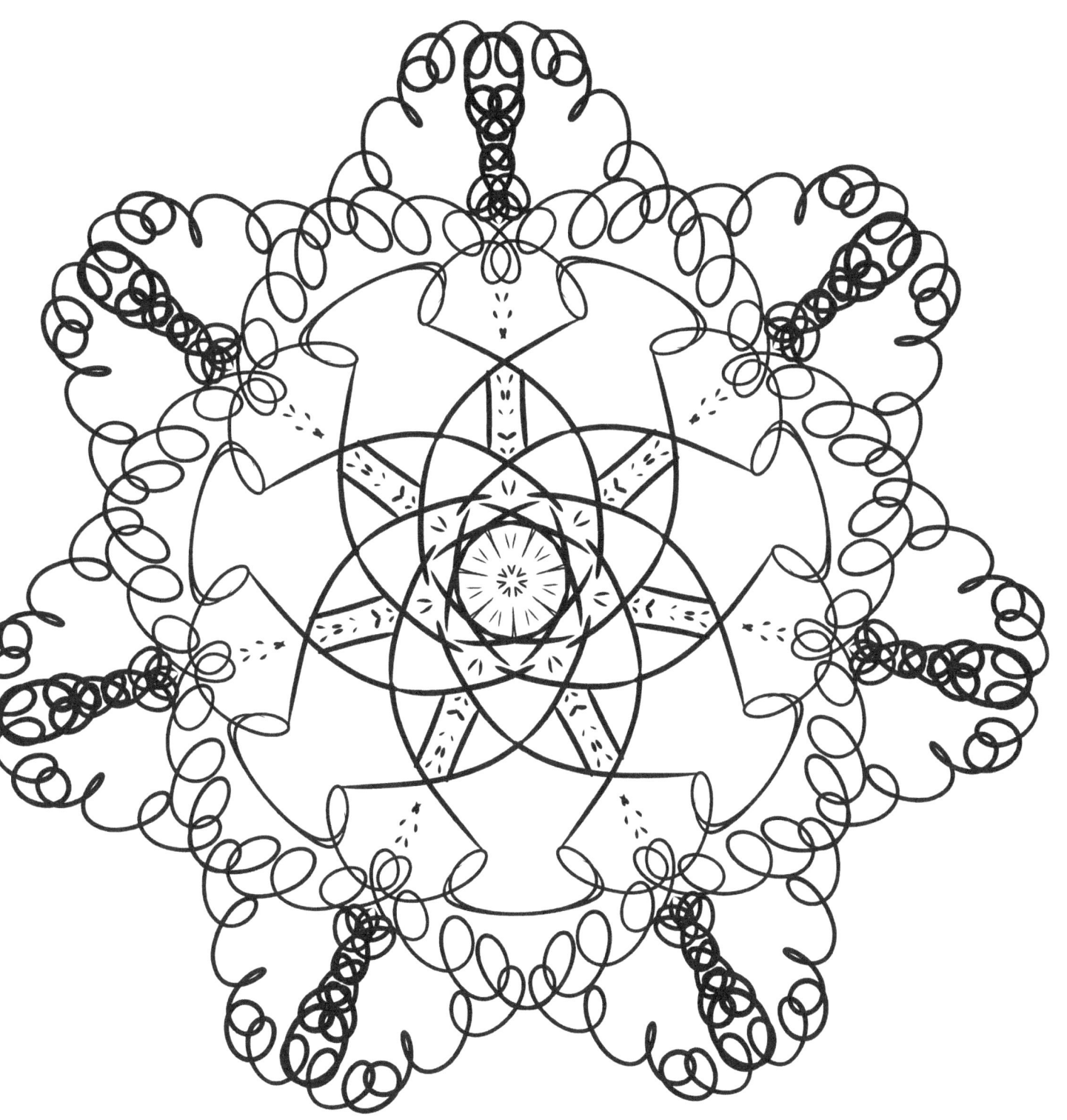

49

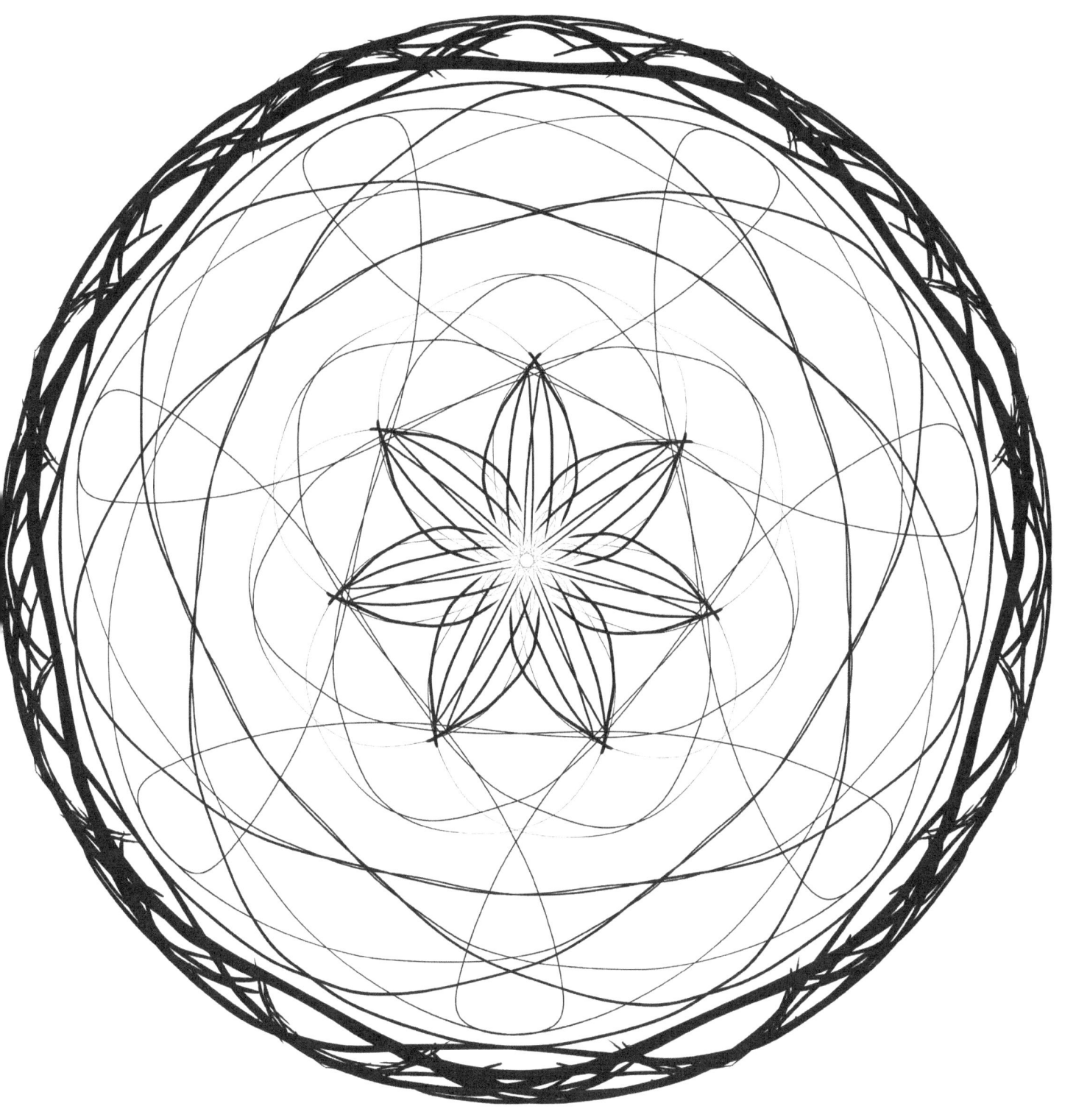

51

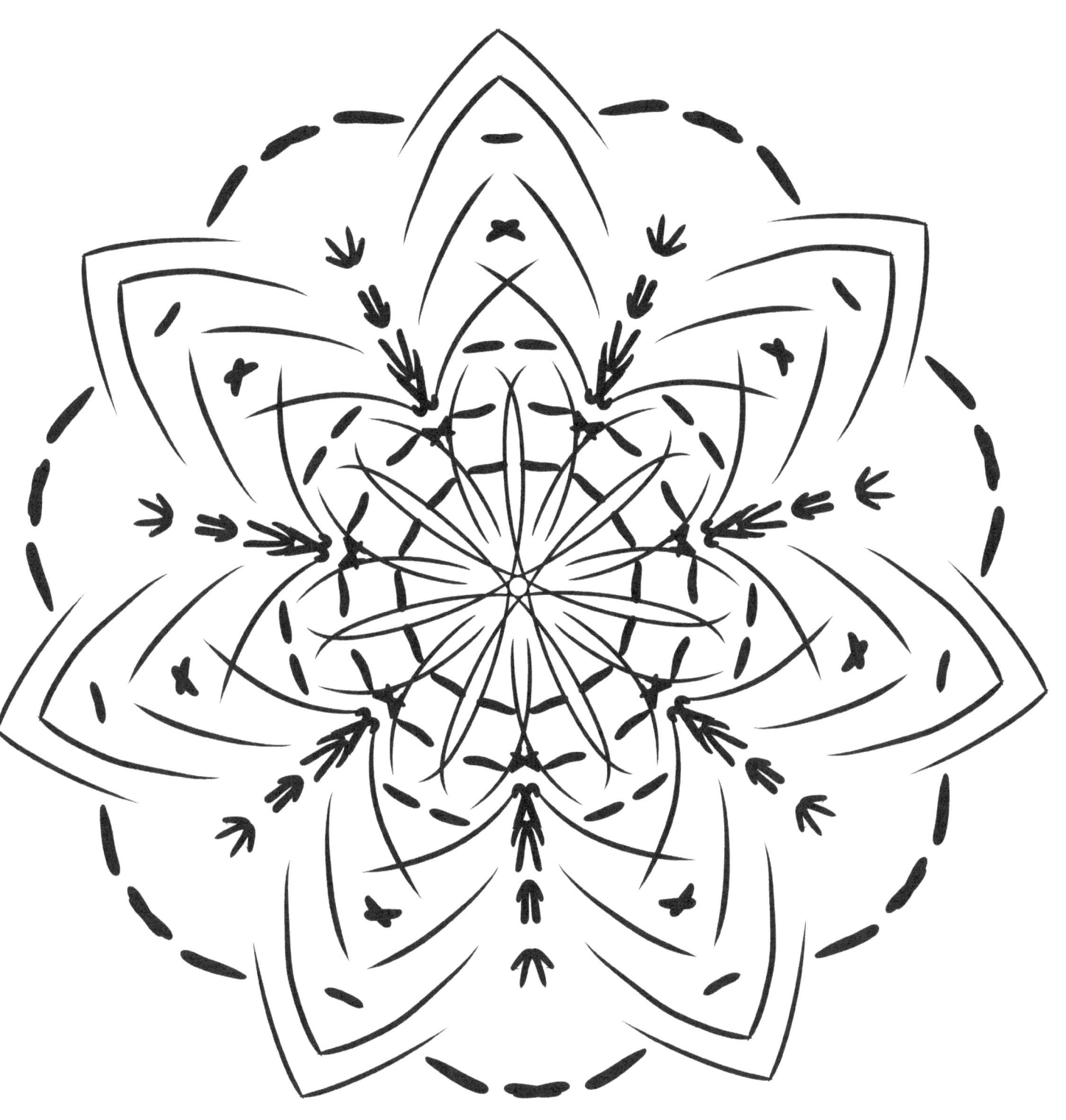

53

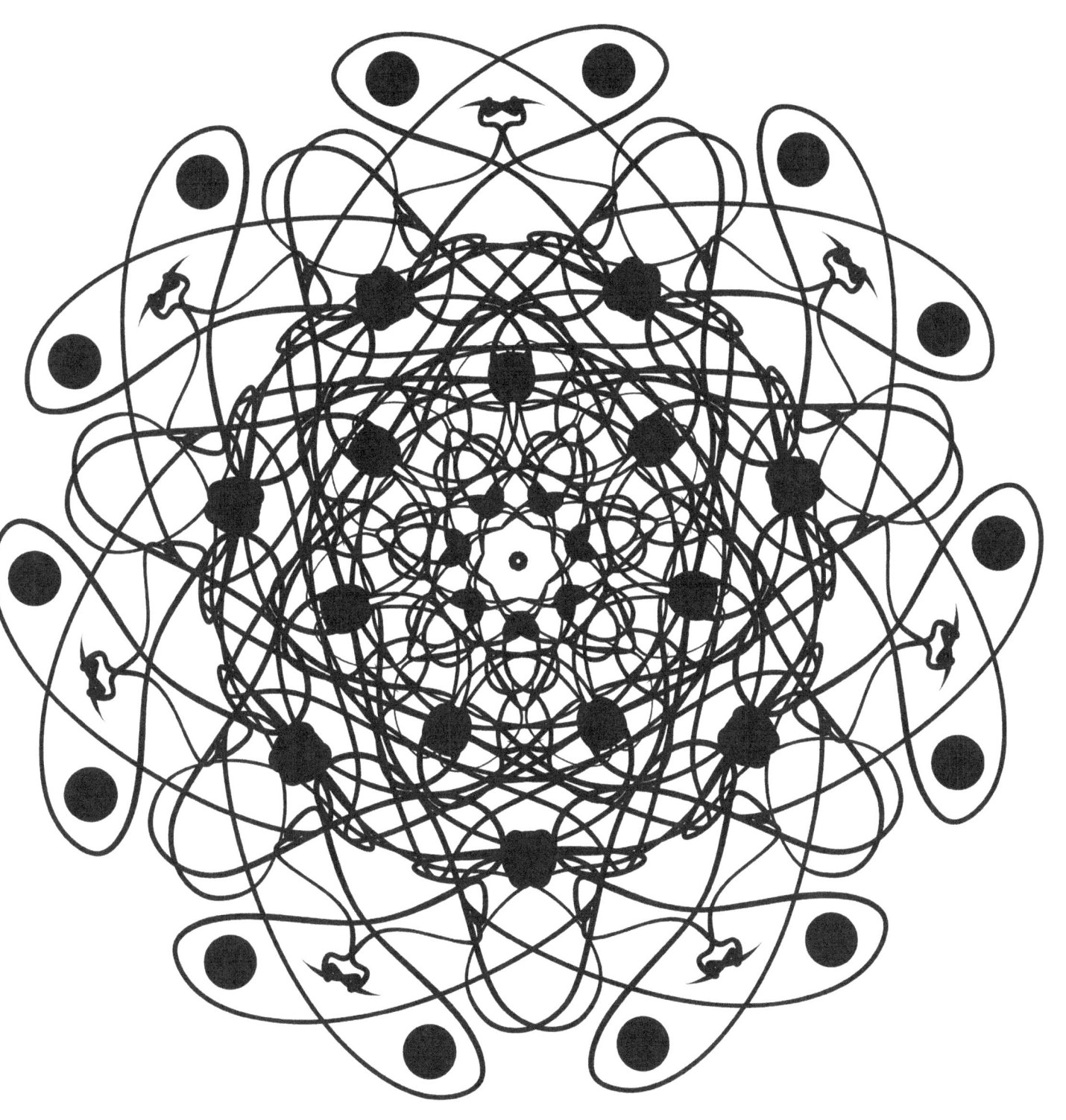

55

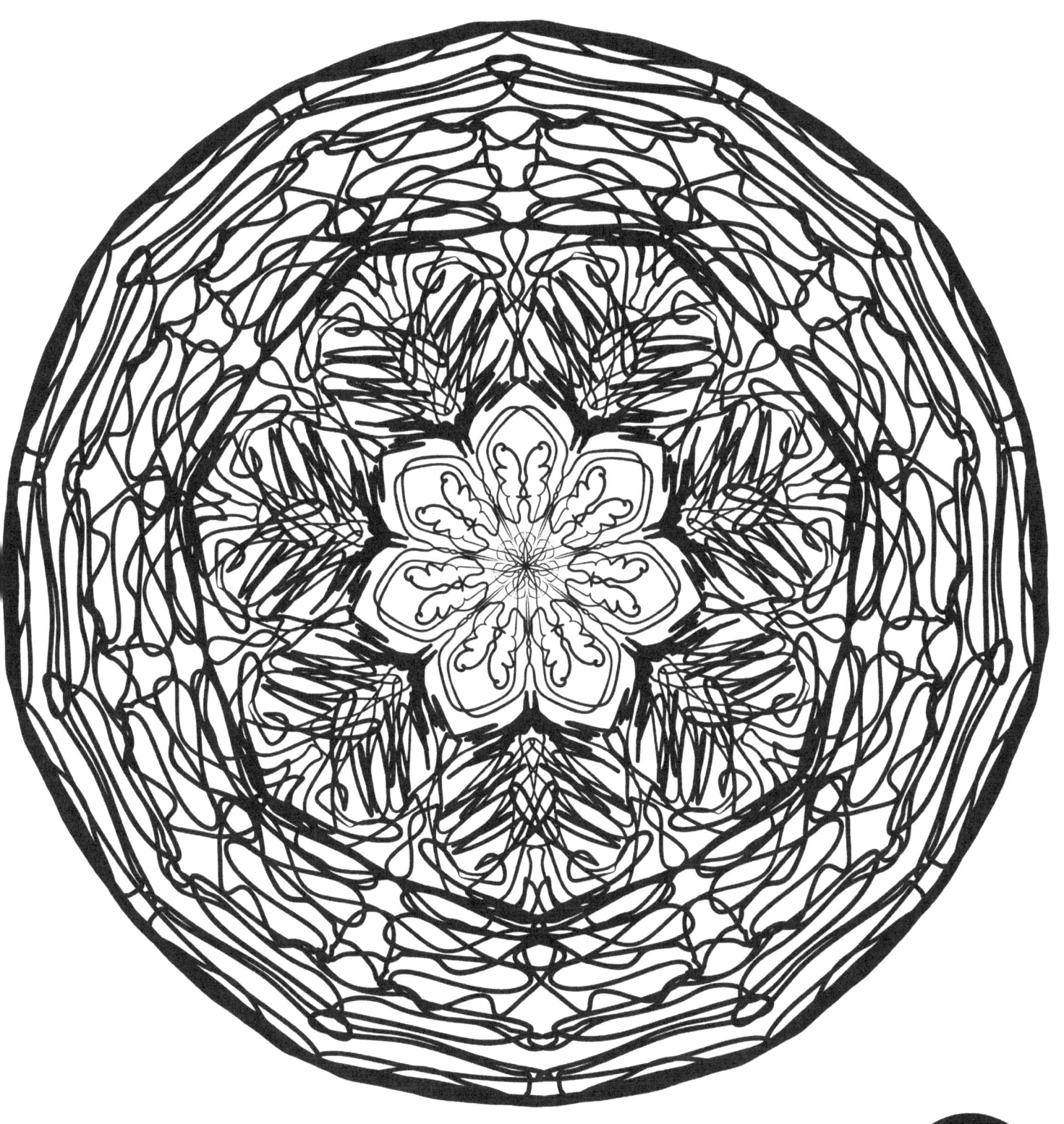

57

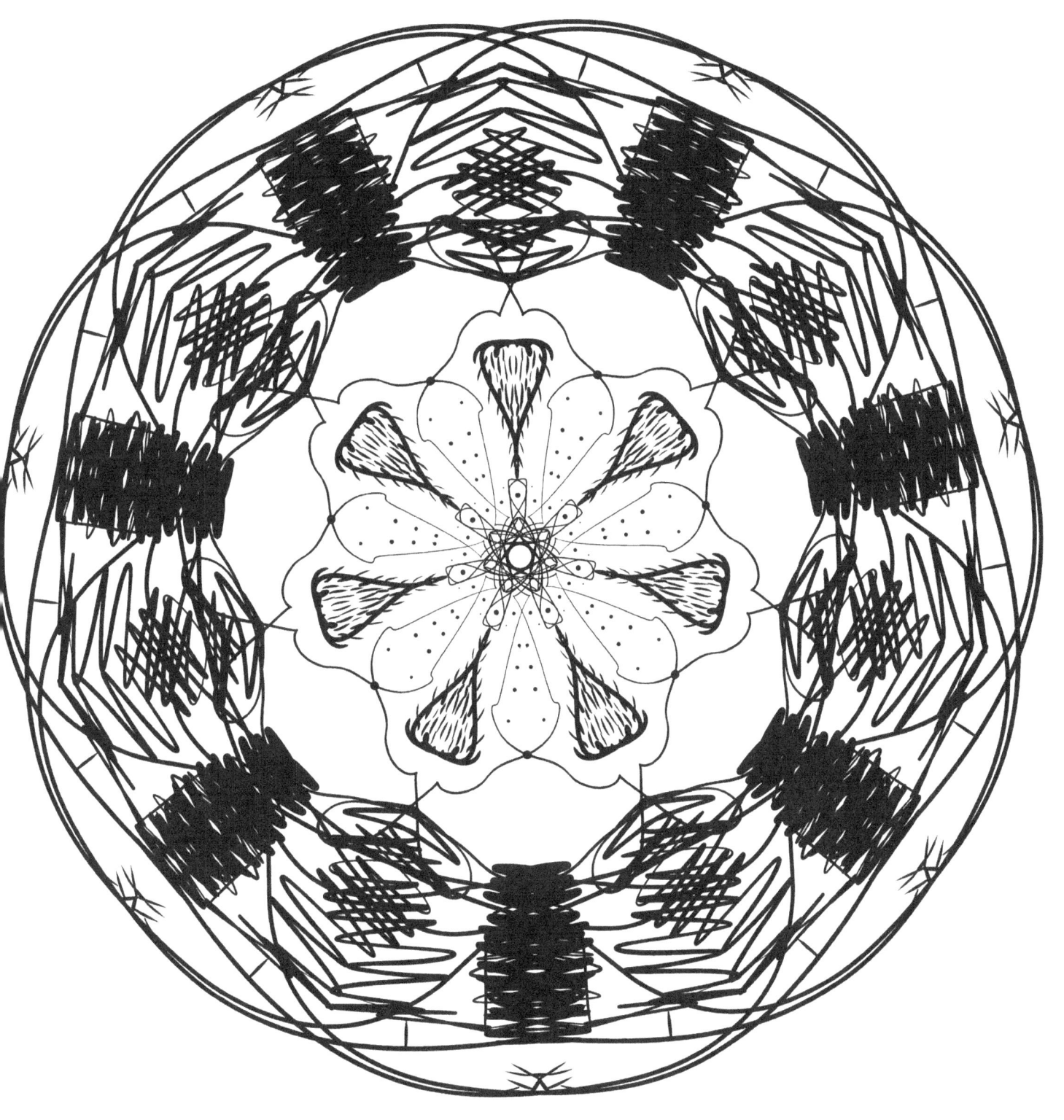

59

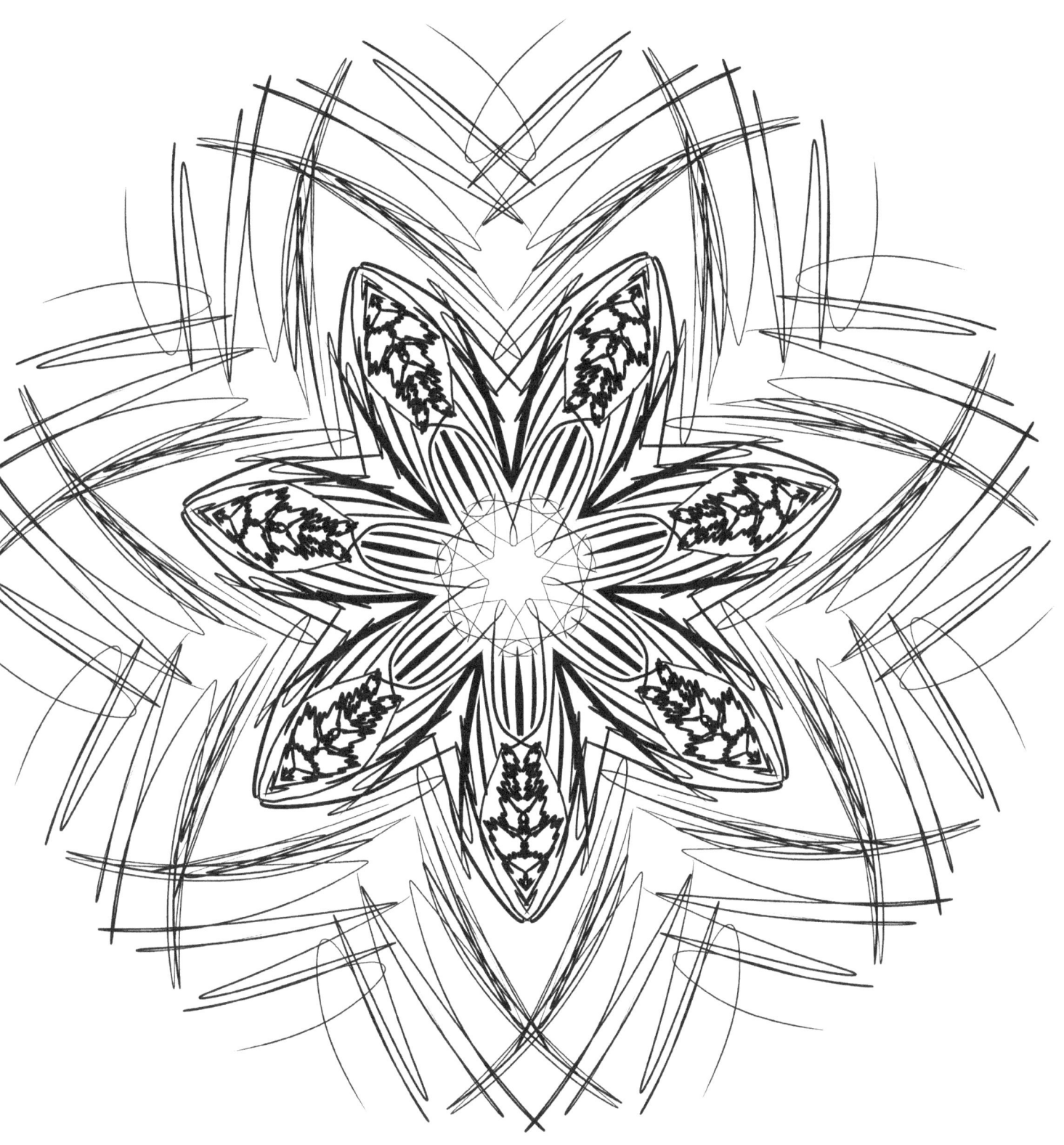

61

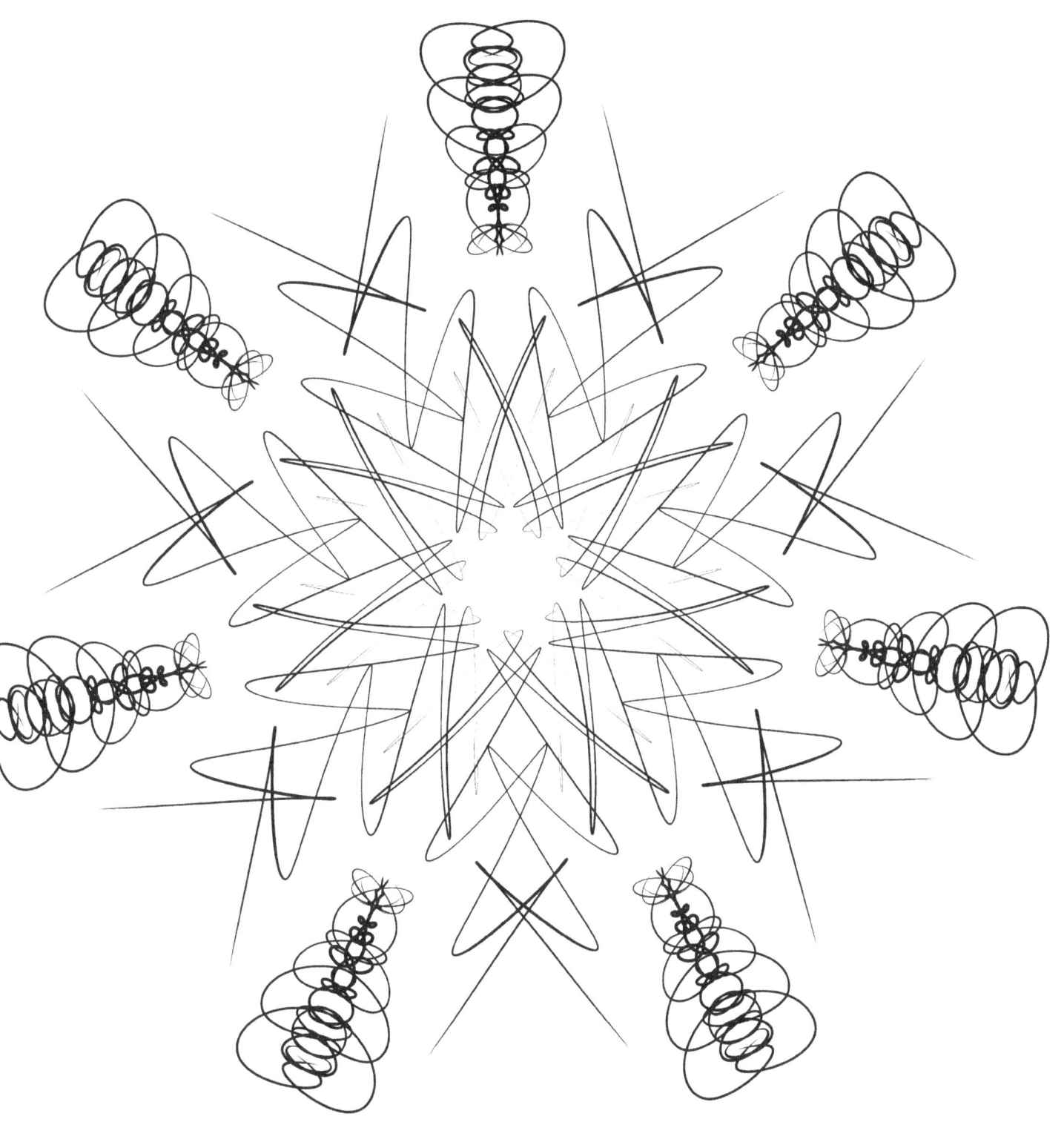

63

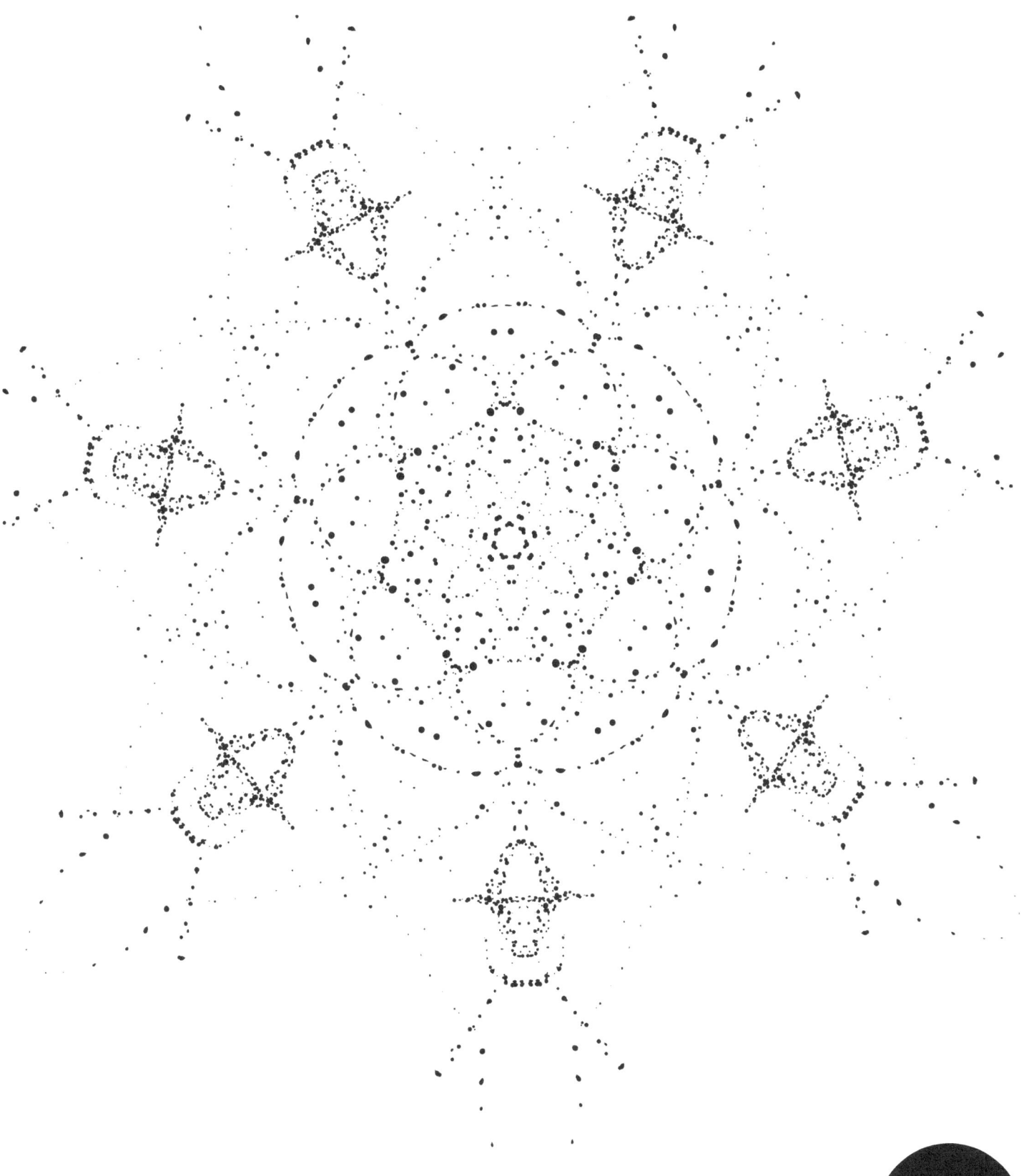

65

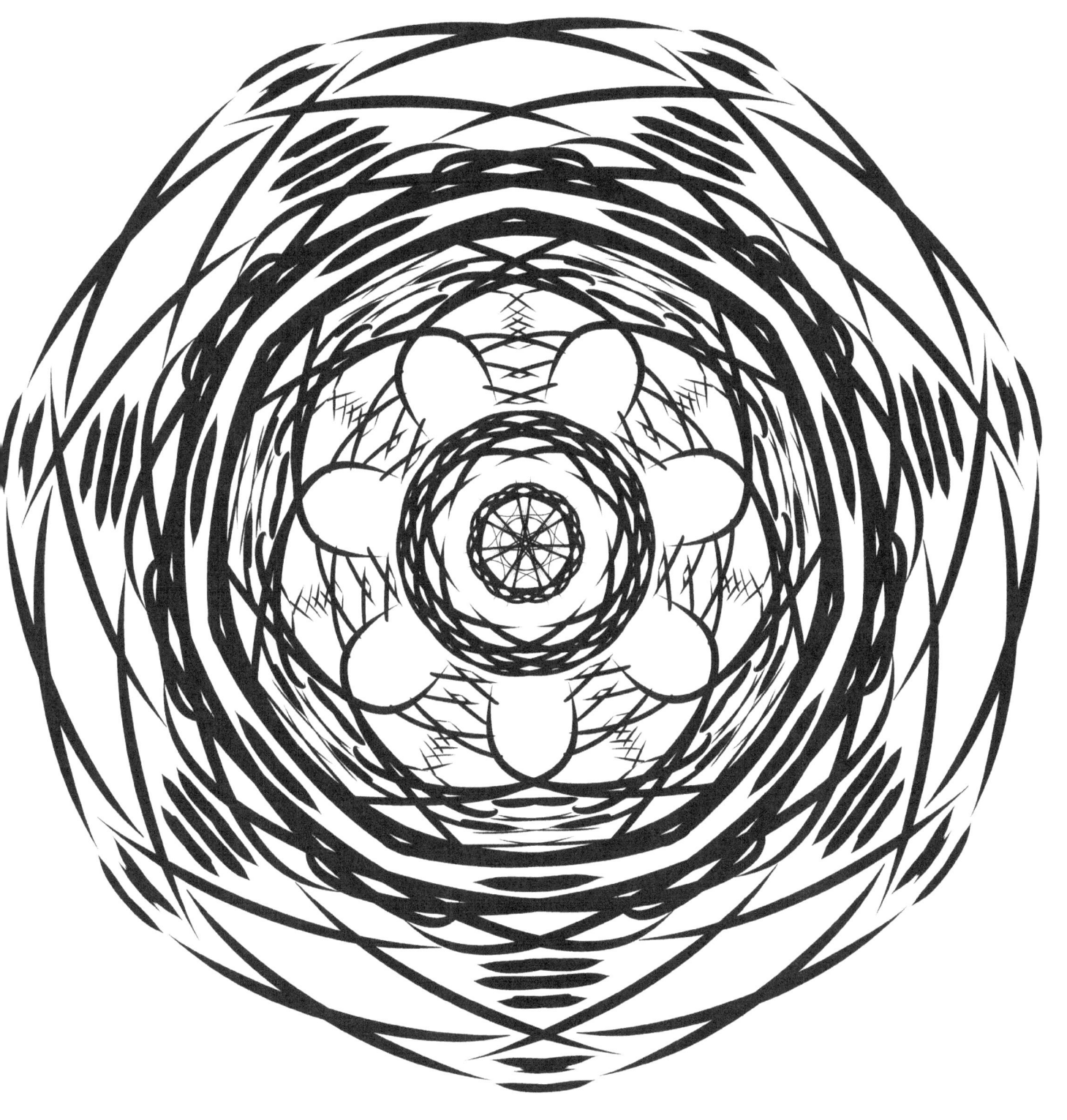

67

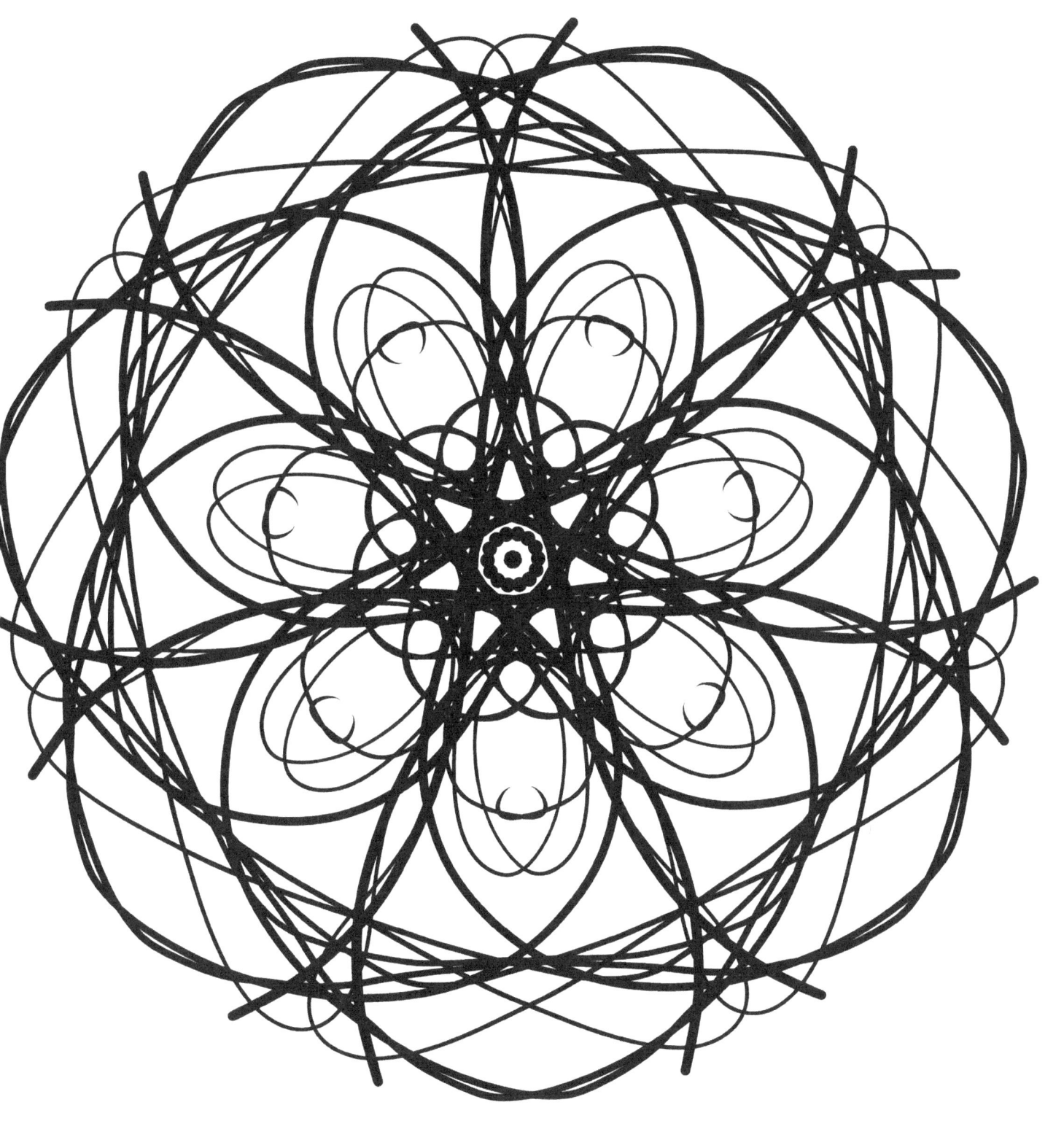

69

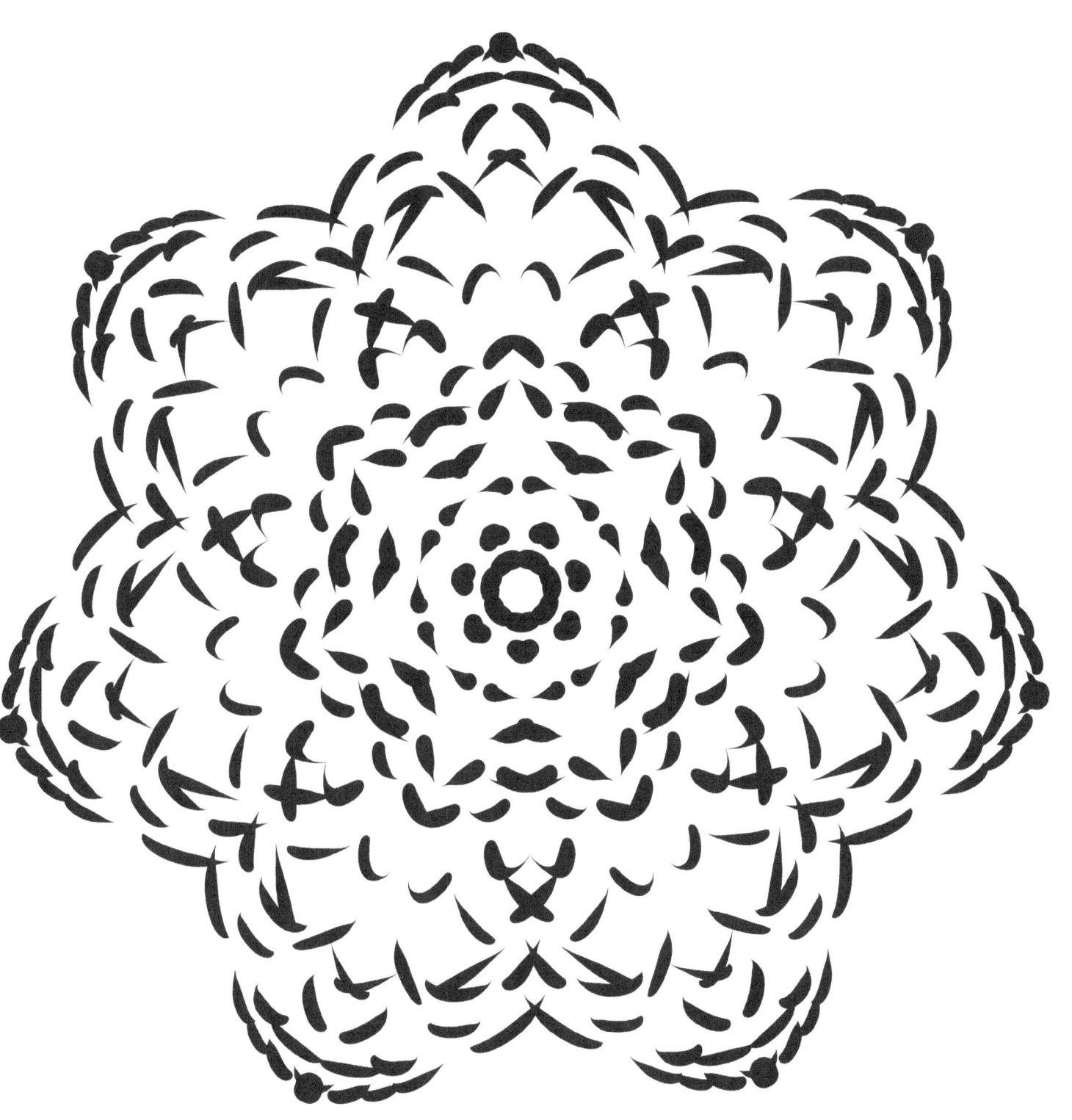

71

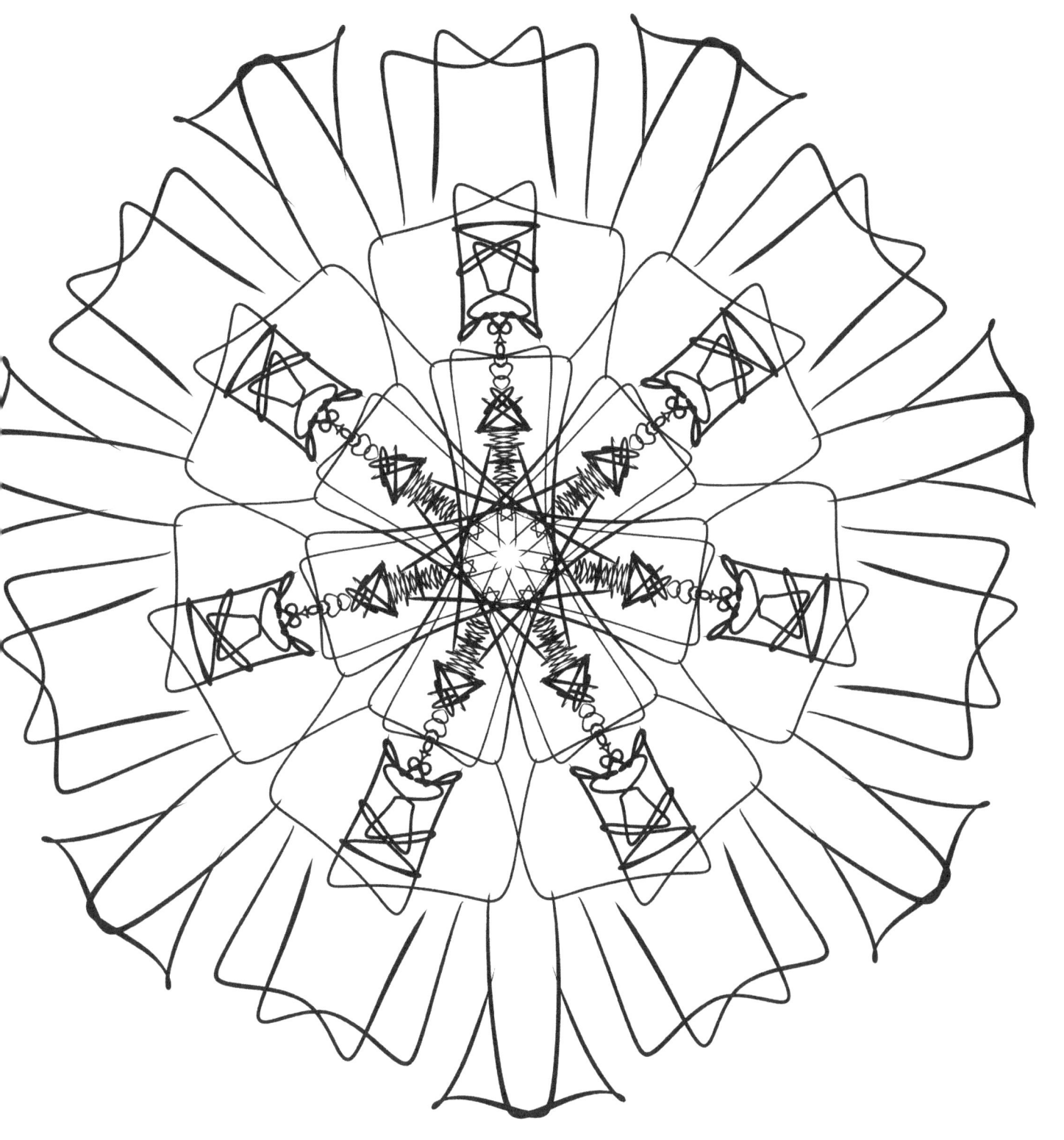

73

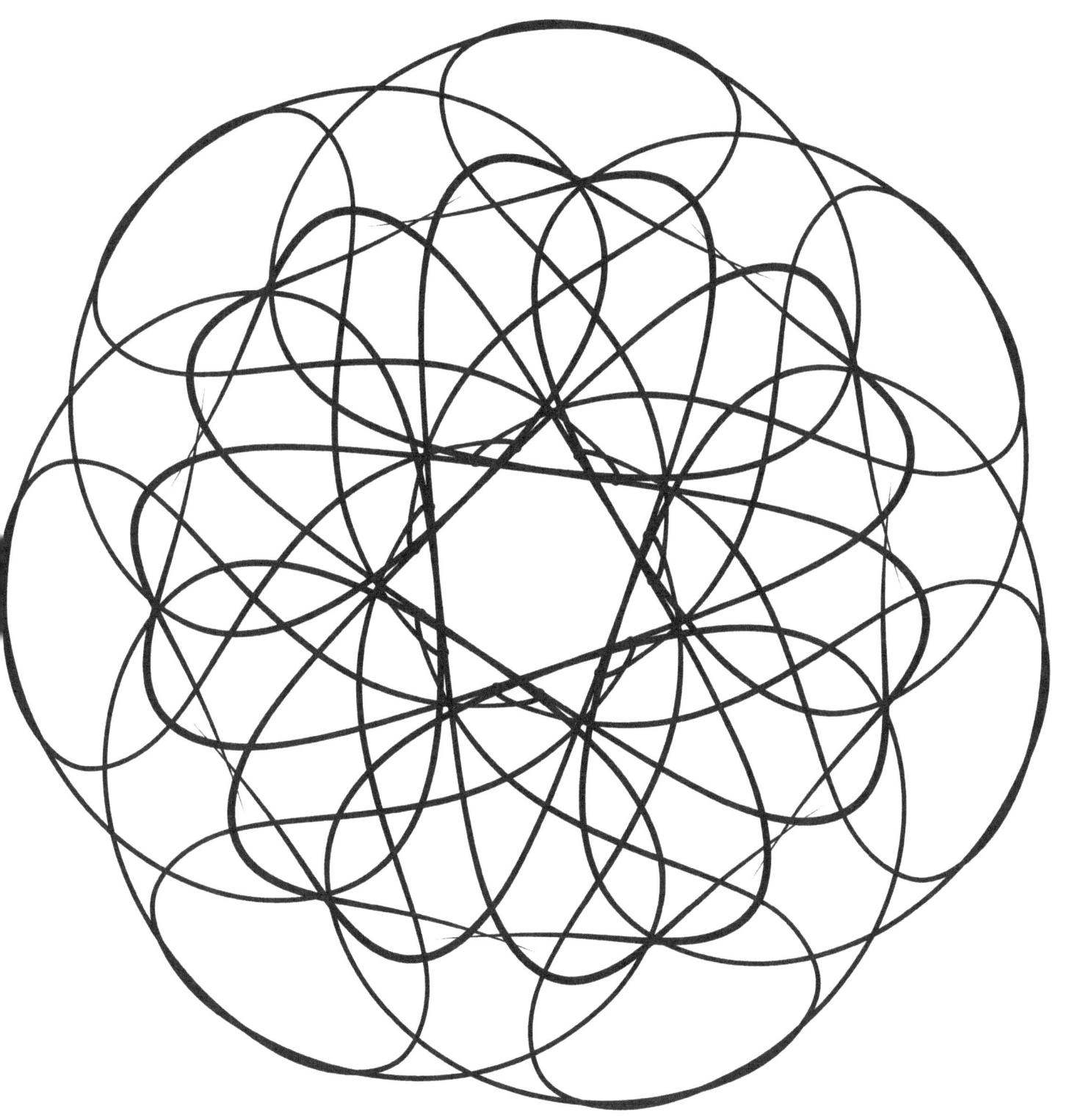

75

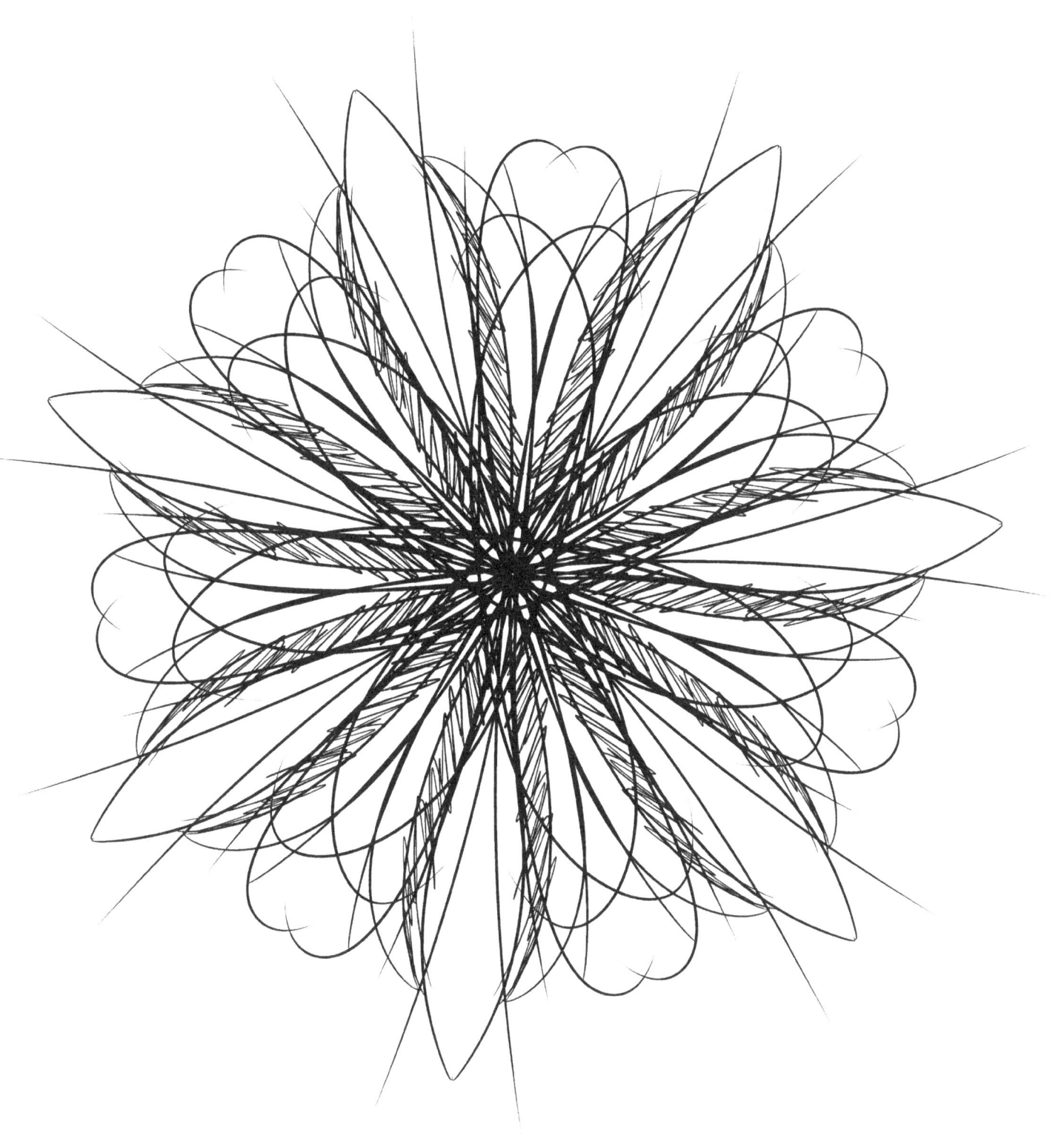

77

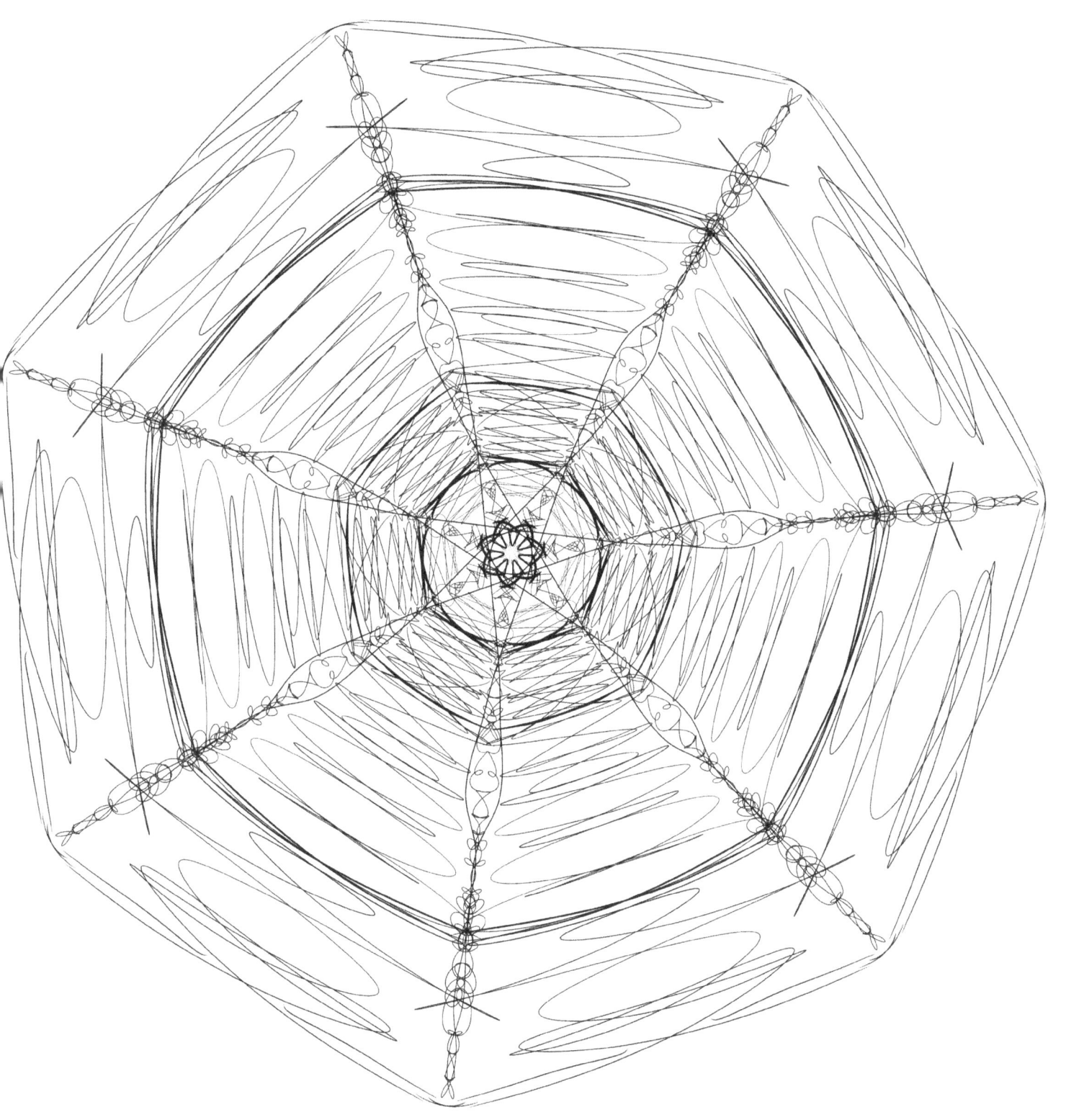

79

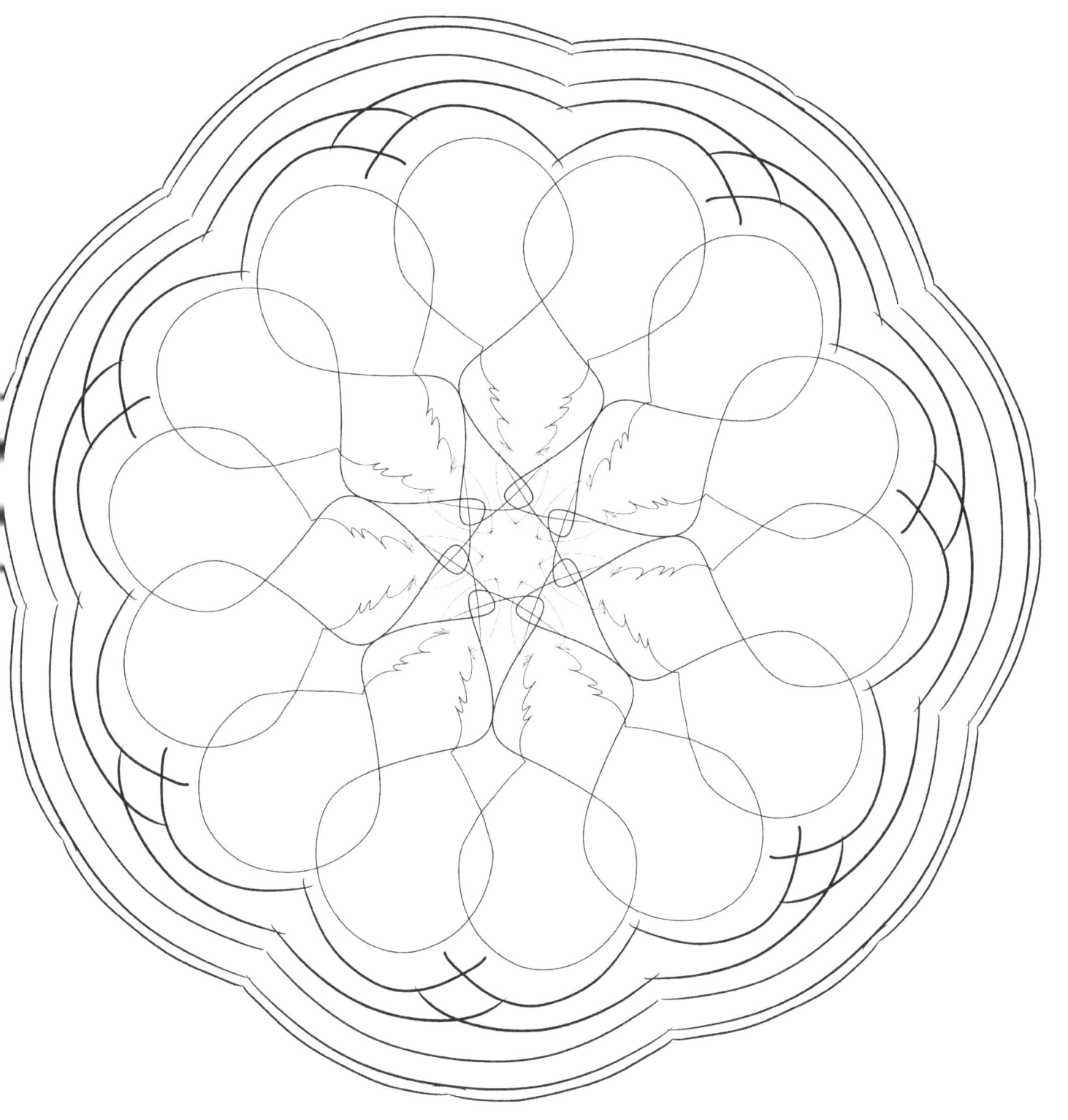

81

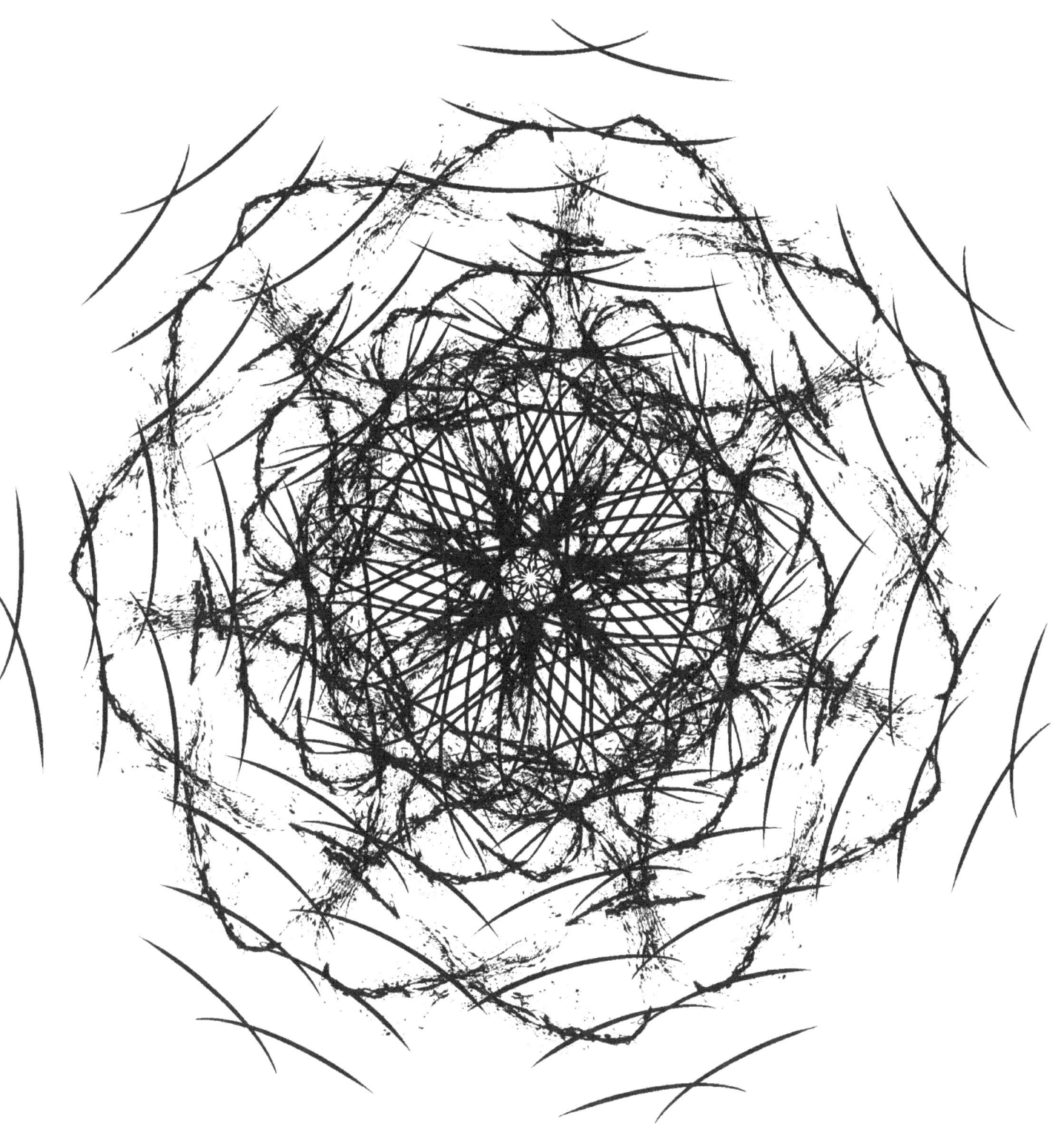

83

www.ingramcontent.com/pod-product-compliance
Lightning Source LLC
Chambersburg PA
CBHW081613220526
45468CB00010B/2855